THE MAGIC PENCIL

THE MAGIC PENCIL

How a Jewish Art Restorer
Survived the Holocaust

Mikel Carvin

as told to

Barry Sheinkopf

Full Court Press
Englewood Cliffs, New Jersey

First Edition

Copyright © 2012 by Mikel Carvin

Published in the United States of America
by Full Court Press, 601 Palisade Avenue
Englewood Cliffs, NJ 07632
www.fullcourtpressnj.com

ISBN 978-0-9837411-7-6
Library of Congress Control No. 2011942336

*Editing and Book Design by Barry Sheinkopf
for Bookshapers (www.bookshapers.com)
Colophon by Liz Sedlack*

TO FELICE
with my love

ACKNOWLEDGEMENTS

I want to thank, first and foremost, my wife Felice for all her help in digging up the records that form the basis of this book and for putting up with my struggles over it.

Thanks to David Sheinkopf for suggesting the title.

Thanks as well to Roy Lucianna, who read the story in manuscript and offered very helpful advice about providing a subtitle and a timeline.

Thanks to my dear friend Eugenia Koukounas for listening to portions of the story for years and encouraging me to write them down sometime.

And thanks, finally, to her husband and my personal "nutcracker," Barry Sheinkopf, who helped me do just that—and designed and published the result.

TIMELINE

After World War I, the Allies have demanded a heavy price from Germany as retribution for starting the hostilities. This creates enormous hardships there. Poverty and unemployment are widespread. At the same time, by 1933 the Great Depression has seized upon the rest of the world as well, and created an opportunity for the Nazi Party to come to power in Germany.

1933

January 30: Adolf Hitler is appointed Chancellor of Germany.

February 27: Basic civil rights are suspended throughout Germany, allowing the Nazi Party to do away with all opposition. Jews and left-leaning civil servants are ousted from public life; trade unions are forbidden. All positions of authority are henceforth held by Nazis.

May 10: The bonfire—all books by "subversives" are burned. Germany resigns from the League of Nations.

1934

Hitler becomes the Führer, the dictator of the Third Reich, in which people become pawns in the creation of a supreme Aryan world. Confiscation of the property of the "unwanted" finances the building of infrastructure and the war apparatus. Employment rises dramatically.

1935

The purification of the Empire becomes law. Jews under German authority can no longer retain their citizenship or have relationships with Gentiles.

1936

Hitler creates the Rome–Berlin Axis. He is determined to make the country ready to fight in 1940.

1938

March 13: The beginning of Germany's foreign expansion occurs with the Anschluss of Austria, the Sudetenland, and part of Czechoslovakia.

September 29: The Munich Agreement between Britain, France, Germany, and Italy is signed, which offers, as Prime Minister Neville Chamberlain declares, "peace in our time" to Europe.

October 9–10: Kristallnacht, the pogrom against Jews, begins in Germany, executed by Hitler's Schutz-Staffel (SS), the "Blackshirts." A small window of opportunity opens in 1938–1939 for Jews to find refuge somewhere outside Germany.

1939

January 30: Hitler declares in the Reichstag, the German Parliament, that he will destroy all Jews in Europe.

March 15: The German army invades Czechoslovakia.

March 29: Britain and France pledge to support Poland. Hitler occupies Bohemia and Monrovia, and Slovakia becomes a German puppet state.

August 23: Germany and Russia sign the Nazi-Soviet Pact and divide Eastern Europe—the Soviet Union claiming Estonia, Latvia, Lithuania, Finland, part of the Balkans, and half of Poland.

September 1: Germany invades Poland.

September 3: Britain and France declare war on Nazi Germany.

September 17: The Red Army invades Poland, *November 1–2:* Germany and Russia formally annex Western and Eastern Poland.

1940

April 9: Denmark and Norway fall to the Nazis after Germany invades.

May 10: Germany invades The Netherlands, Belgium, Luxemburg, and France, after Brussels is bombed in early May.

May 27: The evacuation of British and French troops from Dunkirk begins (it is completed on June 4).

May 28: Belgium surrenders to the German Army.

June 14: The German Army enters Paris.

June 22: Vichy France under Marshall Petain signs an armistice with Germany and is divided into two zones.

July 10: The German air force launches the Battle of Britain.

1941

March 1: To facilitate their efforts to conquer the world, Germany, Italy, and Japan sign a pact of alliance. The Germans also create an alliance with Croatian leader Ante Pavelic. He intends to oust the Serbian population of that part of Yugosloavia and create a sovereign Croatia.

April 10: Germany, Italy, and Bulgaria invade Yugoslavia; Yugoslavia surrenders on April 17. The result is that thousands of Jews, Gypsies, and Serbs are slaughtered.

June 22: Germany invades the Soviet Union and occupies Romania. All who oppose the invasion, Hitler declares, will go to concentration camps.

December 7: Japan attacks Pearl Harbor, in the Pacific, and the U.S. declares war.

1942

January 20: The Final Solution—the extermination of all Jews in Europe—goes into effect. Gypsies, Slavs, homosexuals, communists, and all other opponents of the Reich are to be put to death as well. The SS controls the Gestapo, the German secret police. In the ensuing period, 6 million Jews will be murdered.

November 11: Hitler orders the occupation of Vichy France.

1943

The war against Russia turns against Germany. Hitler declares there will be no surrender of any military unit on Russian soil. The German army begins to retreat and, as it does so, institutes a scorched-earth policy. In November, Africa is lost to the Germans, and shipping lanes to Europe are cleared of submarine activity. The Allies advance.

1944

June 6: Allied forces invade Normandy, and, over the next year, a two-pronged campaign by the American and British armies gradually forces the German army into retreat.

1945

May 2: Germany surrenders. The Occupation of Germany and Austria by the Allies divides the territories into three sectors. Part of Austria is occupied by American forces.

FOREWORD

The clock was ticking—minute by minute, hour by hour, day by day, year by year; and then the bell began to chime, and there were very few of us when it stopped, and fewer of us now all these years later— the survivors.

We still wake up with a sense of foreboding and a creeping terror. We are grateful and yet feel guilty that we escaped and so many others didn't. We carry the burden of damaged bodies and minds. None of us is whole—the experience has shaped us, made us spendthrifts or misers, wasters or hoarders, thinkers or doers. There is no free lunch; we have paid our price. But still, even in hoarse voices, we have to remind the rest of the world that such things have happened. Never again.

Part One

DANCING
IN THE FLOWERS

Chapter 1

LATE ONE CLOUDY AFTERNOON in the fall of 1938, I was coming home to the apartment I lived in with my parents in Vienna. It was in the middle of the city on the extension street of city hall and across the way from a famous theater called the Josefstädter. I was seventeen, and the atmosphere around me was very agitated. We—Jews, that is—were all in constant fear for our existence, uncertain of what the future would bring. Adolf Hitler had been Chancellor of the German state for more than five years; anti-Semitism had been widespread through Europe for centuries, on and off, but he and his supporters had reawakened it and fanned its flames, blaming us for the deep Depression that Germany was suffering, and cultivating that hatred among the supposedly evolved inhabitants of Austria as well.

Personally, I had little understanding of these economic realities, but I could see hateful events being perpetrated all around me against my people, and the feeling of physical safety—the feeling I had grown up with and come to take for granted in a civilized society—beginning to slip through my fingers as I heard whispered tales of people being confronted and attacked in the street, being beaten by merciless young men whose venom Hitler and his minions had encouraged.

I realized, as a result, that I had to escape to some safe place in the world if I were to survive. I didn't know exactly where that would be, but of this I was certain: I could no longer afford to remain in Austria. Each passing day was bringing a noose closer to me and those I loved. I was profoundly confused about how this was to occur, let me hasten to explain—nervous, not at all clear that I had it in me to achieve that goal—but I knew that I must try.

I rounded the corner to my house, opened the

heavy bronze door, and dragged myself down the long entrance hallway with a deeply divided heart.

At the end of that hallway, three corridors extended in different directions. I took the middle one and reached the staircase. We lived on the second floor, the one above the mezzanine, and I had to practically drag myself up those steps in a fog of anxiety. I entered the apartment and called out for my mother.

My growing compulsion to leave Austria needs perhaps a little more explanation, for there were deep family values associated with it. My father had had a military background in the First World War, serving honorably as a lieutenant in the Austro-Hungarian army, tool of the Hapsburgs, and he ran our home on military principles. He never spoke of his war experiences, but they had altered him (as they had so many others) profoundly. In spite of his religious upbringing, he had become an agnostic by the time hostilities drew to a close in 1917, having seen the brutality of mankind at first hand. However, he allowed my mother to more or less run a religious house.

Growing up, I had also often been told, "Money does not belong in your pocket. You will get clothing, food, and an education, but you have to produce accomplishments in learning in order to become an important person in your life." I have never, as a result, allowed anybody to push me around, and the intention of avoiding the possibility of any confrontation like that was the principal force driving me to abandon the newly created Germany (which had been Austria before August 1938, when the Wehrmacht entered Austria in the Anschluss).

I was, as I have said, all of seventeen then, so my idealism (and naiveté) may perhaps be forgiven. It was a time of dualities. Some thought that the Germans would come in and things would get better. Others, acquainted with people who had already escaped into Austria *from* Germany, knew that, if they didn't get out somehow, they would be doomed. It was a time in which even the most seemingly innocent of questions had to be couched in subtleties, whispered in corners, with the SA marching around, listening. Some people who had stores were dragged into the street and forced to clean the public pavements with toothbrushes, cursed and spat upon by passers-by. Jewish businesses had mostly all been shut down and sealed up.

I FOUND MY MOTHER in the foyer; she was crossing to the living room. She was wearing, as always, an elegant dress—this one gray with blue accents. She immediately caught the look in my eye and paused, her lips parted. I sighed and told her, "I have to leave. I've been thinking about nothing else for weeks. I'm terrified, but I have no choice. Otherwise, sooner or later, I'll be confronted. You understand, Mama."

"Wherever you get in the world," she said, nodding slowly, after a long pause, "don't buy anything cheap. Cheap is expensive." Pearly light was falling on the side of her face through a tall window to the left, modeling her youthful features, bringing out the resonance of her deep brown eyes.

She didn't, it was obvious to me, for all that quite comprehend what I was telling her. If she *had* understood what was in my mind, I doubt she'd have let me go. What I had said probably left her in shock; I certainly was in shock. I also had no idea what she was talking about, how cheap could be expensive, or the remotest notion of how such an insight was to guide me as I set out on my own, but the notion stuck in my head.

So I put on my Sunday clothing, which consisted

of a gray wool suit and a white shirt and dark tie, instead of the leather pants I generally wore, packed a few things in a briefcase, gave her a hug and a kiss, and set out for the train station. I had no reason to stay until my father came home from his office, where he worked with my uncle, who was a *kommercialrat*, a sort of commercial counselor, and thus a step closer to the nobility—I had never once spoken to my father except through my mother; by way of reply in such transactions, her sentences to me always started with, "Father decided" or "Father said."

The overcast continued, and I could feel rain in the air. The station was imposing, a big monster of a building with enormous glass roofs and mechanisms. I bought a ticket at one of the windows and took a train to Aachen, a journey of six hours. Aachen, I had heard from friends and through the grapevine, was a place then much different from the Vienna and the monstrous upheavals taking place there. Aachen still exuded organization and calm. People seemed to be living in an entirely other world.

ONCE I GOT THERE, I tried to sniff around, to look around, that is, for what I was seeking—an escape from Austria into Holland.

Two days went by, during which I walked around to see if I could find any information. I slept anywhere; eating wasn't important—one could always grab a roll or something (I had a few coins in my pocket). Upper middle-class people had no contact with this kind of existence. I was already emotionally on the run, already feeling like a hunted animal. It was as if I had been transported to the moon: Every time someone looked at me, my heart stopped.

I went to the railroad station and tried unobtrusively to decipher the schedules of various trains. This took some time of drifting past the posted schedules, pausing briefly, and moving on, so as not to alert eyes to my presence. Whether this made sense as a strategy, I have no idea; whether it was the paranoid delusion of a hypersensitive teenager or, in fact, saved my life for the first of many times in those days, I can't say.

I finally discovered that there was indeed a train that took workers to some factories in the Netherlands, but with my suit I hardly looked like a laborer; so I turned my jacket around with the inside out, bought a ticket with my dwindling supply of German marks, and squeezed onto one of the carriages. It was like a streetcar with benches that ran on either side of a central aisle, very dreary and somehow menacing. Soon the train began to move with a jolt, and we slowly left the city and were soon passing open fields in a continuous drizzle. I was surrounded by dour men in jackets and heavy pants, men with roughly shaven or unshaven faces who fondled white clay pipes in their calloused hands, creatures not unlike those Van Gogh had painted.

QUITE A FEW HOURS PASSED. When I thought I had reached the border of Holland (I don't remember what the town was called), I left the train and tried to get as far away from the station as I could. I walked westward. Night fell, and I crawled under some bushes of a large home and slept the night there. It was a murky evening.

In the morning, an old lady in native costume—skirt and apron—appeared, and started a conversation with me in a language that I could almost translate because it was so close to German. She made a gesture of food with her thumb and middle finger. I replied by gesturing that I would a like a smoke. She brought me a cigarette, and when I lit it, it almost turned my stomach. Much later, I discovered that it was marijuana.

I had thus achieved my initial goal. If only momentarily, I was out of the Nazi grip. I set my goal to get into Belgium and, if possible, Brussels. I started walking southwest.

Chapter 2

ON THAT WALK, THE WEATHER was dreary, misty and overcast, the sort of day that sent a chill straight through one's bones; I had only a vague notion of where I was walking, but I must have crossed the border somewhere between the official posts because I literally bumped into a police station in Belgium—beyond Holland—and, after a less than clear conversation (because they insisted on speaking Flemish and not French with me, and I gave up trying to make myself understood in that language), I was given to understand by the officers, stiff and frighteningly garbed in blue but otherwise quite unmemorable, that there was a train in the station that would be going east. As they led me there, I felt their indifference, perhaps antagonism, and was confused about whether to trust them at all; and, when they pushed me onto a train, I began to sense that their intention was to ship me back to Germany.

I found myself on a typical European train carriage, with a narrow aisle running past individual compartments filled, at that moment, with drab, somehow shapeless people speaking German in a foreign accent, and my suspicion was instantly confirmed: We were indeed bound for Germany—and I was furious that those anonymous cops had been in so casual a position to decide my fate. I ground my teeth together. Panic began to overtake me as the train started to roll.

I slipped into a compartment full of people who, preoccupied by their own conversations, seemed utterly to disregard me, and I managed to get to the window, which didn't want to open completely, allowing only a small space on the bottom for me to just about get my left arm and my head through. At that point, people began to take a mild interest in what I was doing.

With enough squirming, I soon found myself hanging from the outside of the compartment and realized that the telegraph poles were spaced at a mathematical distance from each other, so that, if I were to jump at the wrong m oment, I could easily be split in two. Being a soccer goalie, however, I figured if I passed one pole I could jump through the intervening space before the next could hit me.

I pushed off and—it seemed miraculous, just as I had wildly imagined it might be—landed in the dirty grass siding below the rails, rolling over and over as the train sped on into the distance. I stopped, and buried my face in the ground, and lay there for some time until my heart stopped pounding. The grass was wet, the air still moist and dreary. I finally stood up and dusted myself off as best I could. The ground ran flat as a board for as far as I could see, though the visibility, as I have said, was pretty low.

For a moment I considered what would have happened to me if I had behaved respectably—as my upright father would have expected of me—and meekly taken a seat until the train pulled into Germany. It left me with an eerie feeling of inescapable independence, and I knew in that instant that, for as long as it would take, for as far as I would have to travel, I had only myself, and my wits, and my instinct for judging people and listening to the inner voice of caution or abandon to guide me—for either can, at the right moment, lead to victory in life.

Only much later, long after the struggles I was embarked upon were over, did I realize with something of a start how many people had died, swallowed up in the great greedy maw of the Nazi killing machine, because they had been too cautious at the wrong moment, and how many had died for precisely the opposite reason, daring to swagger when swagger could only lead to disaster.

As I slowly ran my eyes around me at the daunting distances ahead, I figured it would probably impossible to walk to Brussels. I knew which direction the train I had escaped from had been going in, though, so I managed, after a while, to jump onto the last car of a train going in the opposite direction—toward what I assumed must be Belgium. A childhood of jumping onto the ends of streetcars in Vienna, watching the conductor approach and, if he came close enough, jumping off again because I had no ticket, came in pretty handy just then. You have to start running parallel to the train to build up enough speed to make the leap. This I did, managed with a well-timed lunge to seize the vertical iron railing at the end of the last car, and hoisted myself into a position I could maintain. I was winded, breathing heavily, ears pricked like a cat's for any noise that would suggest a human being in the vicinity instead of the hiss of moist wind through my hair and clothing. I hung onto the outside platform of that car for some time, crouching, trying to be invisible and ready to abandon the effort if a conductor spotted me.

One did, and I had to jump off and wait for the next train to come rattling by—again letting go of the train and flying out into space, ready to roll as I hit the ground.

I repeated this procedure a few times more throughout the afternoon and into the night. As I did so, I had a chance, once or twice, to ask directions of people on the road, peasants or whoever they were. I had been blessed with good pronunciation of French by my French teacher, who insisted that you had to convey the language with your lips (he insisted that Germans "spoke with a closed mouth," and that we had to get out of the habit of doing that). It was very helpful, because you don't stand out if you speak more like the natives, you can blend in better, and none of the people I spoke to were suspicious of me. Day and night, I kept on following this plan, leaping onto the end of a train, hiding as best I could until I was spotted, leaping off again, finding some place of concealment until the next train came by, and all the while, whenever I could, asking the way to Brussels.

It was exhausting work, though I was slim and wiry, with good legs and considerable upper-body strength. I ate nothing the whole time and hardly noticed it: I had already by then shoved aside all my emotional responses, and such states as hunger, fear—even the lust to live—had grown distant in my awareness, almost as if they were an irrelevance.

Whether this transformation of consciousness was peculiar to me and stemmed from my own sense of self-preservation, or is common to most or all people in situations similar to mine, I can't honestly say. People imagine that the sudden shock, the adrenaline rush of, say, nearly being hit by a car on a busy city street, the heart-pounding breath that one takes afterward, all of that, is a fair representation of what one goes through (or at least what *I* went through) in a period of extended danger and crisis, but simply amplified. It isn't, not at all. An emotional deadness sets in pretty quickly instead; if it didn't, I doubt that anyone's neurological system or heart could survive the stress.

My concern for my parents continued, however, to be of enormous importance to me, my fear for them. I'd had run from Vienna in order to save my life, in the certainty that the Anschluss would be terrible for me; but it was just as threatening for my mother and father. And if I had managed to generally suppress my feelings in order to better preserve a sense of daring and function, I could not suppress those that had to do with them. My goal in surviving was to survive long enough to help them survive as well.

THE LAST TRAIN I NEEDED to leap onto from a running start in the moist grass of Belgium pulled into the Gare du Nord in Brussels early in the morning about two days later, the weather still overcast and clammy.

The station lies in the heart of Brussels, a big city and, I was surprised to discover, familiar to me, because all the landscapes I had passed through on those trains had given me a feeling of security. I slipped off the back of the train and walked and walked and walked and walked. I slept in a park. I had had by then nothing to eat for three days.

All big cities in Europe have a similar pattern, relics as they are of the walled towns of the middle ages, the star cities that were the cradles of the modern world economy. A center radiates outward; a pace and rhythm of urban existence resembles that of any other city's pace and rhythm. I felt confident in this, my anxiety easing. I slept in a park again that night.

The next day, a young man approached me and said, in German, "You're a refugee like I am, yes?" He must have overheard me asking someone a question. He was of middle height and round-faced, with a mouth set in a continuous half-smirk and thick glasses behind which his eyes seemed enormous, and I could tell from his accent that he must also have come from Vienna. He said his name was Nunio Weitzen. "I heard you speak French just now," he went on. "I can use you. We can help each other, understand? I will tell you what to say, and you can translate it into French, and we can get somewhere in this town. . . . Most importantly, though, you have to clean yourself up first. You're filthy from top to bottom." He brushed me off with great vigor, and wiped my shoes, until I looked more presentable—though I hadn't bathed in four days by then.

He led me to an office building. "We are going to a law office," he said in a confident whisper. "Tell the receptionist you want to talk to the *directeur*."

The secretary and receptionist was a middle-aged woman, conservatively dressed and with glasses on the tip of her nose. Her reaction to my request was immediate, and a minute later a very tall, elegantly dressed gentleman with a thin mustache and colorful tie appeared, eyebrows raised questioningly. I told him, "I've just come across the border from Holland, sir, and my friend Nunio here is helping me, and I'm helping him with whatever I can."

The tall gentleman had bent forward as if to better understand what I was saying, and at the same time I saw his eyes wander from my face to the tops of my shoes, and recognized his gentle smile.

"Could we perhaps provide for you some materials for your office?" I asked, translating what Nunio was telling me in German.

To this he was agreeable. "To keep the price down," I went on, "there should be a substantial quantity of material."

"All right," said the lawyer, consulted with the receptionist, and wrote down a list of materials they needed.

"Could you possibly, uh, please prepay the order?" I asked haltingly. ". . .To expedite matters?"

I could see a slight shock on his face, but then he sized me up again, and his smile became more marked. "No problem," he replied. "We know the prices of the materials. No problem."

He left and came back with an envelope full of Belgian francs, which he gave to Nunio, smiled again, and we left.

Nunio immediately took me to a coffee shop and said, "Now, let's figure this out. You should get twenty percent, and I'll get eighty."

I understood the mathematics of it, but I was utterly unaware what the proportions should have been; I took his word for it and nodded. "Good," he said. "Now let's order some coffee and sweet cakes," the appearance of which made me practically drown in my saliva. The food—cheese danishes, coffee with milk and sugar, flavorful and hot—tasted heavenly, and I felt every bite descend into my empty stomach.

"Let's go now for the supplies and bring them back," I said when it was all gone.

He looked shocked. "Are you *crazy*? What will there be for *us* then?"

". . .I don't understand. You mean you want us to *steal* this money?"

"Call it what you want."

My teeth clamped together. ". . .Where's my twenty percent?"

"No problem." He handed me a pile of bills.

I pleaded, "Please. This nice man shouldn't be *robbed*. I cannot be *part* of this."

"Learn to live with it," he said flatly, "if you want to survive." He tried to convince me, but I couldn't be a thief. I realized that further conversation was hopeless and ran off, back to the building around the corner and into the office.

I asked the receptionist, "Please, can I see the gentleman we spoke to before?"

When he appeared, I had difficulty expressing myself; I was afraid he'd have me arrested. "There have been. . .complications," I told him. "I cannot explain too well, but here's some of the money you gave us. I'll make sure, when the time comes when I'm able to earn some money, that I pay you back everything that has been lost."

He again sized me up, and a bitter smile played over his lips. ". . .Right now," he finally told me, "you need that money. I wish you well—and I'll be here whenever you come to pay it back."

I was totally confused by this first experience I'd had of a financial interaction between grown people; I was also utterly unfamiliar with any organizations that occupied themselves with immigration into other countries from Belgium, unaware of any kind of activity to which I could attach myself in order to move on, any way out. Growing up isn't easy.

Chapter 3

AFTER THAT, I BECAME a wandering Jew moving from one end to the other of the streets of Brussels, admiring the city on the one hand and, on the other, looking for a means of associating myself with somebody, to create some security for myself. In comparison with Vienna, Brussels felt like a small town, more countrified, less sophisticated, the spirit of the people more intimate and engaging.

In addition to that, though French was understandable to me, I was still looking at that entire world as totally strange—an alien planet. I didn't know how to approach it. Could I do whatever had to be done to stay alive—and whom could I ask? The idea of going to some Jewish organization simply did not enter my mind—probably because, though I was a Jew, I had had no education in the religion, so the thought of allying myself in that direction never occurred to me. (My parents hardly involved themselves in it. We had never attended synagogue. My father, though he had at one time actually been trained for the rabbinate, had since the end of the Great War become an agnostic; my mother had made us aware of the various holidays when they cropped up in the calendar, but engaged in none of the rituals.)

I subsisted on rolls I bought from bakeries I passed, and some slices of Italian salami available in the food sections of department stores.

But I had nowhere near enough money in my pocket to put a roof over my head. Instead, I found parks in the city, saw them as retreats, as a haven where I could sleep on the darkest of nights on some bench (it was late fall of 1938 then, a mild spell had settled over the city, and sleeping that way presented no particular difficulty) and, early in the morning, renew my search for tomorrow.

One rainy night, I found that the pews in a church were very comforting, and stretched out on one of them. I also had the opportunity when I did so to make use of the restroom, to throw a little water on my face and make myself a shade more presentable. This was seductive; but, at the same time, I had my arguments with the Almighty. I felt entirely lost, utterly by myself, without a goal in mind or any idea of how to find one. I would have been grateful to do the lowest kind of labor, which would have given me some security and gone some way toward stilling the aimless thoughts drifting through me. But I couldn't approach anyone to ask for a job, that much I knew—I had no identity papers, no way to work legally.

Soon enough, I was arrested, late one afternoon on a street not too far from the Gare du Nord, by a half-bearded, almost peasant-like policeman who at the same time seemed totally disinterested in me as a person. "Papers," he said curtly, the faint sun aglow on the left side of his face, the right in chiaroscuro.

When I couldn't provide them, he did what he had to—took me to a local police station that reminded me in its architectural character of the city hall in Vienna—Gothic, several stories high, with little towers and much ornate detail in stone. We entered, climbed a marble staircase with wrought-iron railings to the third floor, and I ended up in front of a desk with a very severe-looking fellow, not uniformed but in a dark dress suit and tie. I did not feel safe in that place; the hairs at the back of my neck tingled. I realized I needed some respite from the tension building up inside me and awkwardly asked if I could use the bathroom.

He stared balefully at me for a long moment. "All right," he finally sighed, and pointed toward the back of the hall. I found a door that read *Toilette*, entered, and studied the room from top to bottom. All I was attracted to was one of the windows. Crawling over the sink, I was able to reach it. It opened. I couldn't quite see where it was leading, but I swung myself out into the inner court of the building, found enough architectural detail to seize upon on that Gothic exterior, and cautiously descended, foot by foot, steadying myself by clutching any ridge in the stones I could find, to the ground level and through an unlocked door back into the building.

I could feel sweat trickling down my back, not be-

cause of the exertion but because I was certain someone would notice, that the suited *fonctionnaire* would
wonder what was taking me so long and send a contingent to find me. . .but, miraculously it seemed to
me, no one appeared. The stars were out, but by luck
there was no moon. I pressed myself against a wall
in that dim light and waited for the sound of approaching footsteps on the slickly polished floors.

I heard nothing, though, and, at last taking a deep
breath, hurried down a hallway and through a side
door to the street. I looked both ways, saw no one,
and dashed into the darkness, considering myself
lucky that I hadn't plunged into a dangerous situation, broken a leg, or gotten killed in a fall coming
out of that bathroom window, with all that stone beneath me.

In effect, though, I had managed to go from the
frying can back into the kettle. I still had no way, I
realized with a dull ache in the pit of my chest, no
way at all to survive for more than a day or two before some *other* policeman pulled me in. The situation seemed hopeless. One doesn't typically think of
such dilemmas when one becomes a fugitive, however; one imagines grander ones.

At perhaps 10:00 p.m., I had paused at a building that I was thinking might give me a little shelter—because it had a big entranceway that led into a public hall—when a young woman came by. She looked very ladylike, I thought—fully dressed in a conservative coat and a short-brimmed hat with a half veil set low on a triangular, pixyish face that featured almond-shaped brown eyes above a straight, thin nose and bow-shaped lips that she had painted carmine red. She was wearing a musky scent and struck me as extraordinarily beautiful. She asked what I was looking for.

"I—uh. . .my name is Kurt," I clumsily began. "Kurt Goldner. I'm a stranger here, a. . .a new arrival. I'm looking for a place where I. . .where maybe I could perform some service," I told her. "A place to work, or whatever's needed that I could do. Any. . . anything."

Her chin rose slightly, and her eyes met mine with an immediate gleam of appraisal. They were deep eyes, and there was something amusing at play in them. I was drawn to a beauty mark just below the left one. "Call me Lorraine," she said at last, having reached a conclusion: I could see it in the set of her jaw. "Let me see if there's something. Come with me."

We entered a three-story private residence next door, and she took me down into the basement and said, "I want to discuss this with my friends, all right? We'll see if you could be of some use to us."

She left me there. I didn't know what "some use" would mean, but my initial anxiety had by then been replaced by something else—an electricity I could feel in my gut that I understood without understanding it to mean a woman was noticing me. In prior years, I had more than once been approached by women and had been afraid that I could contract some disease from them.

I was still thinking about this when she appeared with two other women, one of whom, an earthy-looking girl in her late twenties with wide blue eyes, an upturned nose, and very full lips framed by a cascade of blonde hair, asked, "Can you do any cleaning? Here in the basement or upstairs?" She took a drag of the thin cigarette hanging from the side of her mouth. She was wearing a light blue peignoir set— *negligé*, casual in a disarming way (I was overwhelmed by her looks, too, but calmed down instantly by the strictly matter-of-fact tone in which she spoke).

"...Uh, yes. Yes! Anything that has to be done,"
I said, "I can do."

She blew out the smoke and nodded. "You can
call me Nana," she said. They took me upstairs and

Lorraine, 1938

led me through the building—not quite into every
room, but through enough of the place to give me an
idea of what they expected of me. "Unfortunately,"
said the third woman, whom I later learned was
named Colette and whose longish face, fine eyebrows,

and even features made her look a little older than she must have been, "there's no private room available for you. But the basement could certainly be made comfortable enough."

Nana, 1938

"Settle down," said Lorraine as she guided me back to the basement. "See how comfortable you can make yourself, and we'll bring you some food."

I had reached Heaven, I thought after they departed and I was by myself. In a matter of minutes, I suddenly had a roof over my head, food on the way, and the possibility of survival.

There were a sink and a toilet in the basement,

Colette, 1938

but no tub or shower; I figured I could manage, though, without the latter so long as I had a washcloth in my hand, and be very comfortable.

I started looking around the basement for cleaning implements and found brooms and mops, and even several work tools—a hammer, a box of nails, screwdrivers, and screws.

Colette came back with blankets, a pillow, and a shaving kit. "You look very tired," she said. "Take a rest. Tomorrow we'll make plans for the future."

I had by then fully recognized the astonishing beauty of all three. . .and that this beauty was the source of their livelihood. I smiled awkwardly at the thought.

She narrowed her eyes, and the faintest of smiles began to play over her thin, wide mouth. "You don't have to be concerned," she whispered. "We're not going to approach you." The Mona Lisa smile fluttered again.

I can't say I was happy to hear that announcement, but it instantly calmed me down.

THEY GAVE ME A GLASS for washing my mouth when I brushed my teeth, too, and showed me how to sharpen the blade of the razor by dipping it in a glass of water and then rubbing the thus-lubricated edge against the inside of the glass.

. "You have to look respectable, after all," said Lisette, "when you make an appearance anywhere."

Chapter 4

B EING IN THE BASEMENT and told not to worry, that these ladies would require nothing of me apart from keeping the house clean, not even wash their undergarments, was as I have said an odd relief.

Each of the rooms was nicely set up as a sitting space—with a table, two chairs, and a chaise longue—and a cotton curtain that closed off a niche in which sat a bed. They said they would take care of the beds, and that there would be a woman come every third day to remove the used sheets and replace them with fresh ones.

I had finally found a peaceful station for my life,

and I indulged the thought that it was high time to appear again in public as a civilized human being.

The ladies were very private; they saw to it that I got meals at odd hours every day, morning, noon, and night—since there was a continual busyness about the place—accompanied by a few gentle remarks, to which they added hints of where and when I could go about my cleaning work.

"Everything will be good for you," Nana kept reassuring me, her lovely face shrouded by a haze of gray-blue smoke, omnipresent cigarette dangling from her mouth, "and don't, for heaven's sake, worry about any of us, you know, trying to take advantage of you." (By then, I was perhaps tiring of this litany of assurance.) I had long since realized that they were professional ladies, that a constant tide of customers washed in and out of the establishment throughout the days and evenings, and that I was obliged at such times to be as invisible as possible. And the idea that their emotions were limited to their business interests was inescapable.

Weeks passed. I learned to impeccably wash everything I was supposed to, was happy and grateful to do so, and, actually, surprised at myself—I had never done anything like it and never imagined it would give me pleasure to earn my keep in such a fashion.

THEN, ONE DAY, A NOTICE appeared in the mail that notified the "resident of the address" that he had to present himself for a *cart d'identité* application at the local police precinct, which was right around the corner.

I showed the letter to Nana and said, "I have to take time off to deal with this."

"*Alors,*" she replied, "*bon chance!*" and left to tell the others.

I entered the police station and found my way to the upper-floor room indicated in the notice. It was a bare, windowless space with a big desk, illuminated by a green-shaded desk lamp. The personage behind the desk, a man with almost perfectly unmemorable features, the sort that could instantly disappear in a crowd or at a party—aside from a wide brown mustache that made his mouth look just as wide when he spoke—immediately began to scream at me, "I know *you!* You're the reason all the windows on this floor are locked, depriving us of a breath of fresh air! You sit down right there and wait for the Black Maria to

give you a ride to prison—and no excuses this time
that you have to go to the toilet!"

It took several hours before I joined a few other
men in the back of a police van, fitted out with niches
in which we were ordered to sit; it stopped quite a
few times to pick up even more passengers.

Finally, we entered a palatial building, huge and
with an inscription above the gate that read *Prison á
Foret*.

After waiting in line once more for some time, I
approached a guard to ask, "Can I maybe have a
glass of water?"

Tall and broad in a blue uniform, he shoved my
shoulder and barked, "Get back in line, you!"

I nearly fell and, in thoughtless reaction, pushed
back. In a moment, he was sitting on the floor.

That earned me a private cell with a meager mattress on the floor and a little bare shelf. There was
no window, just the gated entrance door on one wall.
It was cold, and I regretted having lost my temper
that way. I sighed and sat down on the mattress to
await what came next.

I found a little piece of newspaper in my pocket,
tore out individual letters, and constructed a rudi-

mentary chess set. There are only twenty-six letters in the alphabet, so it wasn't easy to figure out how to do this, but I had all the time in the world, and it helped me take my mind off the foolish, and perhaps dangerous, situation I had placed myself in.

MORE THAN A DAY PASSED, though I couldn't really tell how long it was in the dim light of the cell. At intervals, they shoved a plate at me with meager portions of bread and steamed beans.

At last, a gangly, loose-limbed guard with a thin mustache appeared, rapped on the bars of the cell, and called out, gruffly but in an oddly high-pitched voice, "Let's go. You have visitors."

I said, "I don't know anybody here."

To this came the unfriendly response, "No discussions! Let's go!"

I followed him out. As I entered the visiting room, which was fitted out with a long table separating the visitors from the inmates, I was overwhelmed by what I saw: my three ladies, dressed to the nines, with scarves and fashionable hats upon which flowers figured prominently, their faces pained. All of them began to yammer loudly, in chorus, "*Oh, mon petit chou!* We're so unhappy to have caused you such trouble!"

I calmed them down and said, "You have no reason to be unhappy. I'm only unhappy I can't be in your place anymore," and, after being asked what they could do for me, added that, if they had any pencils and paper for me, I would greatly appreciate them.

Nana found a pencil stub perhaps two inches long in her bag (to this day, I carry just such a stub in memory of those lovely girls—a magic pencil capable, not only of drawing whatever I see in my head, but of conjuring up their unforgettable presence), and a slip of paper that might have measured three inches

Some of my magic pencils

by six. She gave them to me, and as we parted I said, "I will love all of you forever!" Tears ran down their cheeks, and they threw kisses at me.

I took my time in my cell to write a letter on that scrap of paper:

J'etait un elève de 8 á 3 chaque jour de ma vie. Pour souver ma vie, j'áchappait en Belgique. Je ne peaut pas retourner.

A ce moment, j'ai compris que les refugiés plus agées vont ètre transferé dans un camp de detention jasqu'à ce qu'ils vont trouver un pays qui va les permetire a'immigrer—soit Afrique Australie—Asie—n'importe où.

Je vous prie, Monsieur le Directeur du Prison á Foret, faite moi participer á cette groupe. J'ai revè de trouver un place en paix—ou je peut appliquer don't ce que j'ai appris, et surtout je peut apporter mes parents et reformer une famille.

Mille mercis, M. Le Directeur—je serrai reconnaissant toute ma vie. *

*I have been a pupil from 8:00 to 3:00 every day of my life. To save my life, I escaped to Belgium. I cannot return.

At this moment, I understand that older refugees will be transferred to a detention camp until they find a country that will permit them to immigrate—it could be Africa, Australia, Asia—where is unimportant.

I beg you, Mister Director of the Prison á Foret, to allow me to be part of this group. I have dreamed of finding a place in peace where I can apply everything I have learned until now, and mainly to bring my parents to re-create again a family.

A thousand thanks, Mister Director—I will be indebted to you my entire life.

Chapter 5

FEW DAYS LATER, I was let out of my cell to join a group of other prisoners who had been assembled in the prison courtyard, a huge cobblestoned space surrounded by bleak gray walls without the slightest hint of color or human feeling. Each group was kept separate during our daily hour in the open air. I had learned at some point, from another member of the Jewish refugee contingent of a detention center, that some prisoners had been taken to a place called Merxplas.

This time, we were led to a bus that we were ordered to board and that immediately pulled away from the prison. I felt that we were a bunch of trash being taken to a dump. Nervous chatter in which I could not partake, as of old people babbling to each other, was going on all around me. It was still 1938.

IN A MATTER OF HOURS, we arrived at an empty, Gothic-looking gray building with a dormered mansard roof. The place was indeed this Merxplas of which I had heard.

In Belgium, vagrants were arrested, imprisoned in this complex, and made to work for a period of time before being released again into the communities from which they had come. But the building that housed them appeared to be only one of a number of others in the complex. I was never able to become familiar with the rest of the buildings; I and the others in my bus were segregated to only one.

The interior was huge, with high ceilings, and utterly bare. The walls were whitewashed, the floors bare cement. Past this enormous space lay the bedrooms, long, narrow spaces with cots on each side, perhaps twenty to a room, two deep on each side of a corridor. At the far end, a small door led to the toilet, one on each side. Since the doors didn't reach the floor, it was easy to tell whether a space was occupied.

I found myself totally displaced by nervous tension, not knowing what would happen next. It seemed as if I was going from one alien place to another. No responsibilities whatsoever had been laid down by the authorities who operated the facility—we didn't have to engage in labor, for example, to pay for our upkeep. We were simply being kept away from the remainder of society. This state of affairs could easily have caught us in languor, thrown us into a stupor of inactivity; but, immediately, the more mature among us began to create a democracy, voting people into positions of responsibility and organizing the rules of life in the community.

I could not partake, as I have already said, in the conversations that went on among these men, or in this planning. No one paid any attention to me; I was still a kid, and they were all experienced adults with an understanding of the world I did not, it was clear to me, possess.

Everything was indeed organized, though: cooking, sleeping, and planning for the future by inmates teaching trades to others that would be useful for earning a living in some foreign country. There were meetings for engineers and lawyers, people with various kinds of doctorates. In time, these trades included farming, automobile repair, tailoring, and so on.

I finally came across some charcoal in the garbage, bits of wood that had survived the fire in the stoves and been discarded with the ashes, and some sheets of off-white paper (I have no idea what their original purpose had been) larger and heavier than writing paper, and began to draw life-size caricatures of the VIPs among us—like the president sitting on a low stove, surrounded by guards, and of people functioning in that reduced semblance of a broader society. I sketched these drawings on the wall, too—a barber threatening his customer with a knife, a trio of very bookish-looking men trying to learn how to repair a car from a mechanic who views them as hopeless cases, and so on.

One day before breakfast, as we were washing up and brushing our teeth, one of these inmates, a man who was then calling himself Joseph Fabry, started talking to me. He was a graduate lawyer, he told me, and an author who had had many short stories published in Vienna. He had a prominent nose below small eyes that sparkled behind round, wire-rimmed glasses, short hair brushed back, thin lips above a strong chin, and was utterly unimaginable without a suit and tie. "I hope to get an invitation," he told me, "to England. I have some contacts there, and a way to make a living. . . . You're a fine artist. If I get any book contracts," he added, "I'll get you a job illustrating them."

SOME MONTHS LATER, THE MERXPLAS experiment was functioning pretty well socially. The day rooms were comfortably heated, and we all had enough to eat.

Fabry initiated the idea of creating a performance that would highlight the various talents among us and that could be shown to the elite society of Brussels and thus perhaps acquire financial support for the various training programs the leaders of our small democracy hoped to expand.

I created backdrops for this performance, which went off rather well and was attended by a large audience. A ballet dancer from the Vienna Opera appeared, and a chorus. I again found some charcoal and wrapping paper, and created more serious drawings: a bearded religious Jew reading a sacred book, holding his forehead with his left hand and his chin with his right. Apparently this work so impressed a very prominent oil importer that he bought it. (I saw

The Oppressors 1, Merzplas, Belgium, 1938

that drawing several times, when I was already at the Academie a year later, hanging in their living room in an important frame.)

A very strict man called me aside during the performance and said, in French, that he and I would need a translator in order to communicate. I told him, "That isn't necessary. I speak French."

He had many questions. Where had I studied art? I said, "Nowhere. I've never had time to study art,

The Oppressors 2, Merzplas, Belgium, 1938

because I had to go to school."

"Let me see if I cannot follow a thought," he said, "that could possibly be of great importance to you."

I asked in astonishment, "What do you mean?"

"Well, here's what I'm thinking. I will apply to

The Oppressors 3, Merzplas, Belgium, 1938

the King of Belgium to grant you—as the only for-eigner ever to be so recognized—a scholarship to the Academie des Beaux Arts."

I couldn't believe my luck.

A COUPLE OF WEEKS WENT by before I received a note instructing me to present myself at the Academie to be tested for acceptance into the program. The thing still sounded almost impossible. I had no shoes, no shirt, or any other accouterments of respectability. I cleaned myself up as best I could and borrowed pieces of clothing from anybody who would lend them to me—among whom two secretly homosexual men figured prominently.

Outfitted thus, I received a one-day pass from the administration of the complex that allowed me to travel to Antwerp by bus.

Once I got there, I did not feel at a loss, because I was a city-bred boy who knew his way around metropolitan spaces, asking a few questions here and there of people on the street and translating the an-

The Oppressors 4, Merzplas, Belgium, 1938

swers, which were delivered in Flemish, a old style of German that I could more or less understand.

The place did not convey the sense of being a capital city as Brussels had, though as I have said even Brussels seemed like a small country town compared to Vienna; Antwerp had been a great port city during the heyday of the early European capitalist adventure of the sixteenth century but had, by the time I first saw it, settled into a quieter life, a bit left behind by the modern world. Trade neighborhoods, like the one that contained only people who in one way or another dealt in diamonds, lay all over, functioning much as they had for centuries; clothing manufacturers (perhaps too grand a term for those who employed seamstresses with needles and thread instead of modern machines), shoemakers of sorts, all had their districts. The pace of life was even slower then than it was in Brussels, sleepier.

I finally found the walled-in establishment I was searching for. After checking my references, a guard, a simple guy with hair sticking up high on his head, told me, "The director has the flu and has not come in today. Come some other time."

". . .I'll come back later, then."

He shook his head. "You don't understand. He won't be in at *all* today. Come tomorrow."

I traveled through town, looking at and admiring the old-fashioned houses with a lot of red brick and the narrow, cobblestoned streets leading to more generous boulevards.

I came back about three hours later. The guard's eyes went wide when he saw me. "How did you know?" he exclaimed. "He just walked in!"

He took me into the building and said, "Up that flight of stairs, turn left, and you'll find him."

I found a tall, heavy man with the bottom half of his face buried in a scarf; he was still wearing an outer coat with the collar up.

"You speak Flams?" he asked.

"I prefer French, please, if you don't mind," I told him.

"All right, then," he said abruptly in French. "Take that drawing pad over there and draw that vase of flowers in the window."

As I have already said, I have fallen into the habit over many years of keeping the stubs of pencils on my pockets; they have served me well—and perhaps created a kind of magic for those who see what emerges from them. But then, I truly believe, all pencils are magic: They enable us all to leave a record, a testament of our passions, for those to come.

I quickly began.

Chapter 6

I T WAS A SMALL GLUED PAD, and there were a few sharpened pencils beside it. I picked up the pencil and was flooded by childhood memories of when important members of the family had to be shown my graduation papers from high school. Since they, however, had no other way of communicating with me socially (they were prestigious people unaccustomed to speaking to children), they usually said "draw this" or "draw that." I looked at the vase, and my interpretation of flowers as a dance began to emerge from the pencil point, and every tilt of the petals was a motion, and it continued as I danced with the pencil over the paper.

I was done in minutes. He had been walking around, puffing and snorting in his scarf, and taking peeks at what I was doing, the whole time.

Then he called in an old man in a shirt and worn trousers, set him down in a chair, and said to me, "Do him now."

Before the pencil drew a sketchy outline, he turned the other sideways and said, "Now. This way." Even before I was finished, he added, "This is good enough. You will hear from us. Good-bye." His cold was so severe, he didn't even attempt to shake my hand.

I RETURNED TO MERXPLAS SOMEWHAT disheartened— I would have liked a more positive immediate reaction—but there was nothing to be done for it.

The first person I saw was Fabry. "So what happened?" he asked excitedly.

Before I could even try to answer, a number of other people peppered me with other statements:

"How wonderful for you!"

"So glad something positive is happening in one of our lives!"

My description of what had actually happened, however, remained vague and uncertain. I had nothing to tell them, partly because everything had been left in limbo and partly because I had been so enchanted by the drawing task that everything else had vanished from my mind.

Only much later did it dawn on me that I wouldn't even have had the examination if I hadn't foolishly ignored the guard's assurance that the Director's flu would keep him out of the office all day.

A FEW DAYS LATER, A MESSAGE arrived that I had indeed been accepted into the Academie Royal des Beaux Arts. The thing that overwhelmed me in this, actually, was the *exclusiveness* of the royal scholarship, since I was a foreigner: They'd made an exception for me.

Overjoyed yet in a sort of trance, I said my goodbyes to the men at the camp. Joe Fabry left at the same time I did—with his permit to travel to England. I wasn't to see him again for over fifty years. And as I bade adieu to the others, I was struck again by the profound class distinctions among those men— by how awkward former board members of companies, doctors, and lawyers were when they had to learn to wield a screwdriver or bring bowls of soup to a table.

I wished them all well, packed my bundles together, received some donations of clothing and various official papers, including offers from people to become my patrons, and one that assured me a final *carte d'identite* would shortly arrive. I also had a small amount of money on me still.

I SOON REALIZED THAT THE scholarship covered both tuition and materials, and that the patrons would supply a stipend to cover all of my living expenses during my studies. It had been, I told myself, somehow ordained by a benign fate—not that I was entitled to it but that it was meant to be, and my heart truly lifted for the first time in months. I was finding my way out of the mess I had been in since leaving Vienna and becoming integrated into a more normal life pattern, able to function with a certain dignity, to be a man among men, with a goal in his heart, for the first time in many months. . .*maybe.*

I was, naturally, happy to leave the camp, but I also realized that I would again have to find a new place to live, a roof over my head, and a place to sleep while I was studying.

I went back to the Gard de Nord, with which I was by then somewhat familiar, and started to hunt for a place I could call my own.

I RAN INTO A GRAY-HAIRED WOMAN with a very square face, somehow reminiscent in her angularity of a Van Gogh figure, wearing *sabots* and carrying a pail of water and a scrub brush, who was washing the sidewalk in front of small whitewashed stucco building. I asked, "Would you have a room for me to occupy?"

She said in Flemish, "Yes, there is one, all the way on the top of the building."

Steps meant nothing to me. I asked her how much it cost, and she gave me a price that would have been a third of my stipend. I had to ask further questions about whether there was a kitchen or a bathroom or anything else. "Is there a bed in the room?" I asked, which surprised her.

". . .Yes," she nevertheless said, "I suppose that can be arranged."

She showed me the room. The ceiling had a forty-five-degree slant to a row of horizontal windows. The walls were painted an off-white, and all I could see from the windows at that odd angle were clouds. There was a single bed with a blanket and pillow but no sheets. There were a few other pieces of furniture in there too, a primitive table and chair, and an enameled cast-iron heating stove in a dark reddish-brown that was completely disconnected. At once, the question of where the toilet and bathroom were located became crucial. I paid her and asked where I could find the bathroom. "It's on the floor below," she told me.

"Is there, uh, a key for the toilet?" I asked.

She said, "There's one on the inside, but not on the outside."

So for the first time, really, I started to face the daily challenges of living a private life—continuously confronting needs and figuring out how to overcome them, needs my mother had always met for me and that I had never been aware of: where to buy food and what to buy, things like that. I was surprised how easy it had been to find that space—it seemed like a coincidence, as indeed it was.

By then, the late-summer light was failing, and I settled down, spreading my little possessions all around the room, and prepared myself for my first day at school in the morning. I was enormously excited and hopeful that I would be able to associate with other young people. My only concern was my inability to speak Flemish, which I perceived as a stumbling block to a successful future and wanted to learn as quickly as possible.

AFTER A LONG NIGHT, JUST after dawn, I got out of bed, washed and dried my face in the bathroom, and hurried down into the street. I found a big street clock near the Gare du Nord that gave me the time. It was six-thirty; my classes would start at eight. I stomped into life like that, without attachments, with all my strength before me. . .as Benjamin Franklin had two centuries earlier, except that *he* had wisely tucked three freshly baked rolls under his arm.

As I approached the Academie, I found a boiling sea of young people engaged loudly with each other. It instantly and unexpectedly made me feel very inappropriate, a stranger to youth and exuberance and, basically, the joy of living. I had no connection with them whatsoever, I realized with a shock—boys and girls more or less my age but with normal lives, well fed, housed in clean homes and with loving parents around them.

In a cowardly fashion, I slunk away from them and murmured to myself, "Maybe tomorrow will be better."

It took me four days to force myself not to run off but to stay.

Chapter 7

I MUST REMIND THE READER THAT, at that moment, World War II *had not yet begun.* I was hoping to read in newspapers of promising events—that Hitler had receded, or disappeared, that Fascism would somehow vanish. There was a depression in Belgium, part of the worldwide collapse that had begun nine years earlier with the crash of the stock market in New York, though I of course had no inkling then of this latter truth. I read that England, through Neville Chamberlain, was trying to play a mediating role with Chancellor Hitler. The extermination of the Jews was not even widely, to say nothing of univer-

sally, known, though *Kristallnacht* had already occurred in Germany. There was some incident—Jews,
I recall, going into the German consulate in Paris to
take revenge for what was happening—though the
details will no longer gel in my mind. I was very worried about my parents, keeping up a constant stream
of letters of encouragement between us, praying for
good things to happen; England and the United States
ranked as guardian angels in our minds. (This image,
of course, was totally obliterated as time passed; we
all have a selfish outlook about the future.)

This was the historical background—foggy, uncertain, driven by incomplete information and
rumor—to my life. The personal struggle I was going
through at that moment was sharper, more acute: I
was living in an alien city in which I planned to acquire an education in fine arts, yet afraid to go to my
classes. I cowered, deeply lacking in confidence. The
hours ticked by.

I eventually steeled myself to attend classes,
where, as timid, or frightened, as I was, I was very
collegially received by my fellow classmates. They
saw me as just a little different from them, but they
totally accepted me as I was. This came as an enor-

mous relief. The girls in particular seemed very welcoming—very Belgian, very Flemish girls, and a few Jewish ones. There were also two Dutch boys—one, Jonny Horeman, already had a manly appearance, with whiskers under the nose and on the chin; the other was Pieter Braat, long-haired, blond, more boy-

Fellow student Jonny Horeman, Antwerp, 1940

Fellow student Pieter Braat, Antwerp, 1940

ish looking, and the owner of a guitar that greatly attracted me—who accepted me immediately as a comrade and said they would go back to Amsterdam with me if necessary.

I found out from my teacher—a square-built, important-looking Belgian gentleman, very accommodating in speaking French to me instead of Flemish, and willing to throw a German word into the conversation as well here and there—that I needed to buy all kinds of material to work with. When I asked where I could get them, he said there was a shop on the ground floor of the school.

I took the list and went there immediately. When I entered the shop, it was filled with students. It was a very businesslike setting, with a businesslike approach. Shelves, running to the ceiling on the gray walls, were packed to overcapacity with materials of all kinds. There was a crowded space before the counter, filled with young people chattering away. The noise was overpowering, and the place smelled gray and impersonal—one would have thought of turpentine and chalk, but I don't believe there was any of that.

When my time came, I handed the list across the counter to a somewhat neutral, robotlike fellow in a white smock. Everything was already known to him. He asked no questions but immediately proceeded to build a pile of materials on the counter—pencils, canvases, drawing pads, watercolor paints, tempera, and so on. As he prepared the package, he howled numbers in a loud voice, and I realized with a shock that he was calling out prices, and that what I had been asked to purchase amounted to three-quarters of my stipend.

All I would have needed to do was give him my scholarship number, but with all the kids around me I was too stupidly embarrassed—overcome by my father's warning never to accept gifts for fear of winding up on some corner with a hat out, begging for coins! Four years earlier, my class in Vienna had gone on a skiing vacation into the mountains, and parents had been asked in a note to give us money for the trip, which I handed to my mother. The next morning, she told me, "Papa said no." I hadn't questioned this decision, had gone to school and told the teacher that he had declined. The teacher had told me, "Without you, this excursion will lose its enthusiasm. We have some extra funds. You can come with us regardless." When I came home and told this, very proudly, to him, my father had said, "Where are you aiming in life? Are you aiming to stand in a corner with a hat between your two hands and asking, 'Please, can I have a coin?'? You don't ask for, nor do you accept, alms!" and gave me an envelope with the money in it.

Overcome, as I say, by this image, I immediately paid for the art supplies, so I wouldn't be thought of as a beggar.

I left the shop, however, desperately wondering how I would pay my rent or buy my food. I would not have looked askance, I told myself, if any of the other students had been in the same position; I didn't have to be embarrassed to be in it. But it didn't matter—"He would not go beyond his father's words," says Robert Frost of a farmer in "Mending Wall"; I understand that well.

On the way home, I entered a bakery, and a lovely, plump, elderly lady in a big apron, with a thin strap around the neck, that was voluminous and must have gone around her three times, asked, "And what for you?"

I asked, "Do you maybe have some old bread?"

"Yes," she said. "One day old."

"Nothing older?"

". . .Mm, yes. There is some that's two or three days old."

"And the price?"

"Much less than half."

The bread appeared—a big round wheel of black

peasant bread, perhaps fifteen inches in circumference, packed in pergament paper, a material halfway between parchment and waxed paper. I felt a definite firmness as I carried it under my arm.

There was a sort of department store as well nearby that had all kinds of food for sale. I finally acquired the cheapest but largest can of sardines in tomato sauce I could find. I came home and developed a practice that has remained with me ever since: I cut the bread into thin slices and smeared the tomato sauce over each slice, wrapped each piece in a portion of the original paper, and ate a slice, cut in half, at each meal.

Whenever there was a lunch break at school, all the kids came out of their classes and sat down in a stairwell or the lobby to eat their lunch. I usually had a girl sitting on either side of me. "What kind of meal do you have there?" asked one, a blonde, short-waisted Jewish girl with a lovely oval face who was exhibiting fine signs of mature development that I had already developed the x-ray vision to appreciate, so that I mentally undressed her with my eyes (as I did every attractive young thing I encountered in those days). Let me call her Mariette—I can't recall her actual name. She was the daughter of a diamond dealer who asked me to come to synagogue with him during the High Holidays, principally so he could go out and smoke. I knew I shouldn't on such a day, but he insisted, so I did. . . .

"Something special," I said to Mariette.

"It can't be special, because you had it yesterday."

"No, no. This is different."

She finally said, "I think that my friend and I would like to come to your kitchen and do some cooking for you."

My abode, of course, didn't have a kitchen, stove, sink, or anything else. I vehemently refused. "It would be totally misunderstood by everybody, and I couldn't permit that," I explained.

MY DAYS WERE FILLED WITH excursions into the art world to try to prove my value as a student, expressing myself as an artist and exploring all the possibilities available to my talent. A Black American sailor who had somehow failed to make his ship found a job at the school working as a model, and I was struck by the physical differences he displayed in the shape of his head, the musculature, the bodily proportions—my eye acquired a real appreciation of these differences.

I plunged into the sculpture classes too and found I had a knack for representing the human form in

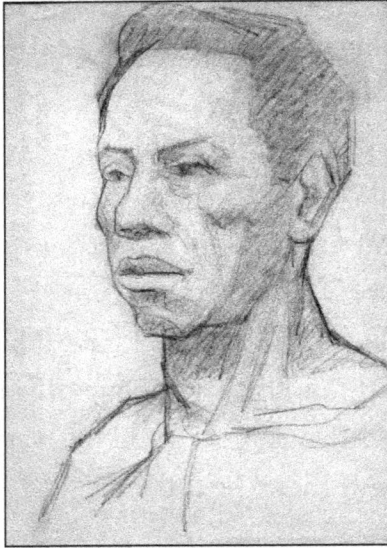

African American sailor, Antwerp 1940

three dimensions. In a modestly proportioned room without many pupils but with brilliantly evocative north light pouring through large windows, we were taught by a short man with a little moustache and glasses who combed what little hair he had over a bald forehead.

After one project, a classic torso of Hercules, the class over, he had gone; I put a portrait of the instructor's head on the torso of the hero. The kids all let out a howl, which suddenly ceased. The room be-

African-American sailor, Antwerp, 1940

came deathly quiet, and when I turned around, I found him right behind me. I expected a punishment of some kind, but all he said was, "The nose is still too small. Add to it, and then destroy the piece. We need the material for our next class."

In this fashion, I studied, more or less theoretically, classes on architecture and on the restoration of oil paintings. I rarely went home. There was always something being taught, and I wouldn't let go, I was so hungry for all of it. I also studied drawing from life models in pencil, charcoal, chalk, and all the other materials available. On and off, one of the models came to the apartment of some pupil. My room was too small for such events, but I was always invited, and there was no charge to anyone. We did more impressionistic work at those gatherings.

Reclining Nude, Antwerp, 1940

Life Study, Antwerp, 1939–1940

All this gave me little time to look for ways of making some money, which my father's pride had forced me to do. First, I was given an opportunity to sort diamonds by color at a jeweler's—Antwerp was, after all, the major diamond center in all Europe. The father of petite, blonde Mariette, a good-looking man in his fifties who had a distinctly British appearance, always in a tie and jacket and coat, had me come over to his shop and asked me whether I could detect color differences in a handful of stones he showed me. I could, and so I spent some days doing so for a little pocket money.

But it was more convenient for me, because it was closer to my home, to work in the bakery. I entered the store and asked the lady if her delivery bicycles did not need a coat of paint. "By all means," she said. "If you can do that, we will be happy to provide good, healthy things for you."

So every time I came back from the Academie, I sat there and painted the delivery bicycles—until one day someone tapped me on the shoulder. I turned around to find my drawing professor, a short, rather plump man with a round face in which a largish nose fought with an incipient double chin for prominence, short-cropped hair, and heavy black-framed glasses, who said, "No wonder you're always too tired the next day. Give up these things! I'll see what I can do for you."

Chapter 8

I GOT A SMALL STUDIO SOMEWHERE in the back of the Academie, where my drawing professor very thoughtfully provided me with canvas and paints, in which I plunged into the spirit of the artists of the seventeenth century—the joyful spirit of expressing, that is, their happy lives. When the Spaniards were defeated by the English, the Netherlanders had turned away from depictions of Christ on the Cross and towards a celebration of their own robust lives— Hals, the Breugels, Vermeer, all of them. They had exalted the ordinary, the humble, the daily life they all lived. They created a glorious testament to the meaning of being human that, in some ways, has never been matched, and certainly never been exceeded.

I painted dancing peasants tumbling over each other in relatively tall but narrow canvases, working in oils, reliving the joy of the freedom they had then achieved. It was like a freedom for me too at one remove, an opportunity to escape, as they had, from the miseries of everyday survival.

After refusing to allow Mariette to cook for me, she must have realized why, and that I needed some form of income. She therefore came up with a proposal for me to teach her something in languages— she wasn't interested in German, and she of course knew French and Flemish, so she came up with the idea of me teaching her English, of which I knew not a word. I suggested that she buy a book on how to learn the language, and that I would try to use it to instruct her. I would read a chapter the night before and then take the bus out to the suburbs, where she lived, to perform my pedagogical best.

When I arrived, her mother, father, and sister all told me how wonderful it was that I had come when

I had, as they were just starting their dinner and would be happy to have me as a guest. The parents were very mature-looking folk, very respectable, and I later learned that the father, who as I have mentioned was in the diamond business, was measuring me at that very moment for the possibility of a liaison with his daughter.

"Thank you," I said, "but I've just eaten." My stomach was in great disagreement with this response. (This was, again, of course, the teaching of my father—don't accept charity from anyone!)

Mariette and I had our lessons in the living room of her elegant home—she in an armchair, I on a Louis XVI brocaded chair, with a little round table between us and a small hexagonal one to the side, beneath a tall shaded lamp. Beyond us, a chandelier hung above a rather striking sofa, my ever-present cigarette trapped between the first and second fingers of my right hand.

I also met a man—stout, vigorous-looking, clean shaven, and nearly bald—who approached me one day at the school and asked me, in what I assumed was a businesslike manner, "Can you paint murals? It has to be done in one week. I am opening a restaurant in Ostend—as soon as you can, I need a mural for it."

"Of course," I said, visions of food and shelter rising before my eyes. "I'd be happy to."

"How much will it cost? . . . Let's break it down," he went on, seeing how unprepared I was to provide a quote.

I said, "Materials might be. . .about sixty-five, and—"

"Times seven," he said, "is 455. And labor. . . ?"

"One week," I said, "would be seventy."

"All right," he said, "times seven is 490, so the whole thing together will cost me 945."

I was flabbergasted and confused, because I had given him weekly, not daily, figures, and I didn't know what to say.

"Vacation time is coming up, I know," he said. "I'll give you a thousand in round figures to include the trip to Ostend, so you can buy your materials now."

This experience was real eye-opener for me. It was then the spring of 1939. The generous interpretation of my estimates demonstrated either my ignorance of business realities or his utter kindness to me, and I imagine an artist with any experience would have charged the thousand—but I had no way of knowing that at the time. It would, of course, completely alter my financial position.

THERE WAS NO PROBLEM GETTING to Ostend, a couple of hours away by train. I was carrying a satchel with my equipment, hoping it would be sufficient to complete the work. When I got to the station, it was a bright spring day, a bit on the chilly side. I asked how to get to Au Cheval Blanc, which was the name of the place, and walked.

I was surprised, when I got there, at how tall the walls of the place were—perhaps twelve feet—but felt challenged at the same time, and made immediate sketches in pencil of what I thought would be appropriate. I saw a landscape with joyous dancers and a little white horse hopping around among them. I showed it to the owner, who just smiled and said, "That's exactly what I expected from you! Thank you. Proceed! How will you squeeze all of it into one week?"

"I'll squeeze in more hours," I assured him, "by using the evenings."

A hundred times a day, I ran up and down the ladder he provided. Since the walls had already been primed with white paint, the tempera I used was easy enough to apply. The room was pretty spacious, and I was expected to cover all the walls. Some of the faces I laid down were life-sized, many smaller as if in perspective, and much of my journeying up and down that ladder involved making sure that the relative proportions were correct. The palette I had selected was joyous, too—white, red, a lot of green, bringing nature indoors.

When the seventh day approached, I was totally exhausted—but so happy to see that huge grin on the owner's face when he came in to see the completed project. It was the first time I ever saw a smile on a client's face, and it had remained with me ever since, as a benchmark for so many others—if I don't see that smile, regardless of the fee I have charged, I honestly feel I haven't been paid, that I have somehow been reduced to the level of a transaction that has demeaned both me and the client.

AT THAT MOMENT, THE UNITED STATES changed its immigration policy and the issuance of its visas. My

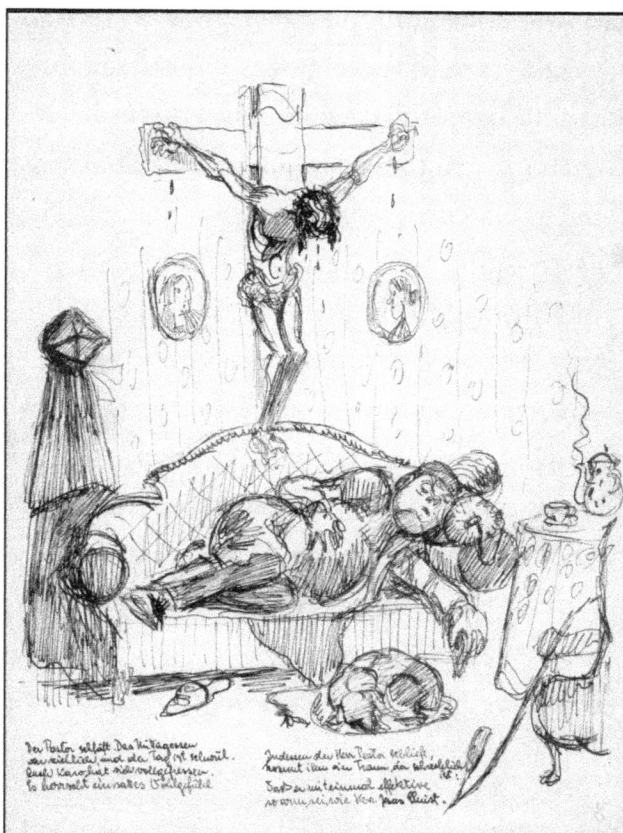

Ironic View of Reality, Antwerp, 1940

sister and her husband had applied for a U.S. visa in Vienna, filled out the forms, and passed the necessary exams. They had been advised, however, that they would need to pick up their visas in Brussels. They'd acquired a transit visa and come. When they applied at the U.S. consulate, however, they were told that they would have to travel to Lisbon instead, and that they would be notified when to go there.

When I heard they were in Brussels, I asked them to come to Ostend, to see my achievement. They did. My sister—tall, well-dressed as usual in a suit and fashionably wide-brimmed hat, a looker I'd had to confront troublesome men over—glanced briefly at the work but was more interested in the fact that there was a casino in Ostend. "Listen," she said to me, "how much have you earned on this project? Why don't you give me the money and let me grow it for you at the casino? I'm really good at that sort of thing."

I did, gave her every last centime. She blew all of it.

Chapter 9

⌒∞⌒

TOOK ANOTHER WEEK AWAY from the Academie; the owner of the inn had offered me a job as a waiter. It took only one day for me to decide that it would be too dangerous for some poor unassuming diner to be crowned by me with a tray or serving platter.

One older gentleman who worked in the background of the restaurant taught me two chords on a guitar, and I sang for the whole week based on those two chords, a D and an A—when the guests asked for a Danish or Swedish song, I sang "Mein Yiddishe Mame."

I returned eventually to school and began to study and concentrate, seizing upon everything the Academie had to offer and working again under the inspiration of the seventeenth-century joys of living.

There were always evening courses on architecture and art restoration and conservation as well, which were barely attracting enough pupils. But I could not let go of any of it, because all of it fascinated me; it was like learning medicine to save the lives of works of art that were ready to dissolve through time or negligence, either on the part of the original artists, some of whom had at times been less than assiduous about preparation of canvases, paints, and varnishes, or of those into whose hands the works had subsequently fallen and who knew precious little about how to preserve them. I felt, as I say, like a doctor. I also painted perhaps twenty canvases of my own, inspired by those jubilant seventeenth-century masters, and occupied myself with the sculpture classes I was taking.

A year thus passed very happily for me; though I was constantly working, I felt myself growing as an artist and a person, able to express the jubilation of my own life.

When my drawing professor caught me painting bicycles, he had also told me that he would arrange a show for me when I was ready. An exhibition space was in the process of being set up on the outskirts of Antwerp for that show, scheduled to open in May 1940.

About six months later, in the late fall of 1939, I had a meeting with one of my donors, who was a Belgian oil importer. His wife had bought some of my pieces at Merxplas, and they had become fervent supporters. He was a very young-looking man, not formal, not at all like my image of an important businessman. I showed up at his office, a very strict desk-and-bookcase arrangement. I wanted to escape, more or less, the machinations of his wife, who was arranging social meetings with her friends to which I would be invited somehow as a sort of personal discovery. I wanted, however, to speak to him, not about this, but about plans for the exhibit and about my wish to invite them to the opening.

He was enthusiastic about this prospect. He took over the position of his family towards me once he realized how pressured the society ladies were making me feel.

The winter of 1939 was a very cold one, and my sculpture class went out and created life-size statues of heroes on horses out of snow. It was adventurous and exhausting and frigid but not to be missed. The whole class had a lot of fun doing it.

WHEN THE EARLY SPRING OF 1940 rolled around, my sister learned that her visas were going to be available in Lisbon, and she and her husband started to prepare for the trip. I slowly moved one painting at a time to the exhibit hall and began to install them, participating in the motions of the dancing figures.

The day of the opening, early in May, after I had worked to exhaustion in the exhibit hall, I rushed to my patron to again invite him to the opening. He was all excited. "Didn't you *hear* anything last night?" he asked me.

"Hear? Hear what? I was tired and asleep."

"You didn't hear the noises of the German army invading this country? . . . I'm terribly sorry, but I can't go with you. I have to attend to my business, you see, under these conditions. But you go ahead— maybe we can do it tomorrow."

I hurried back to the hall and found it smoldering.

When I entered the room, there were my dancers—
surrounded by flames ignited by bombs that had just
hit the building. I could have saved some of the
paintings, but the fire was licking around the entire
room, and the figures actually started dancing before
they slumped into ashes on the floor below, and the
owner of the building, a simple soul with bushy hair
and a mustache that covered his lower face, came in
and pushed me out, crying, "Out! Leave now, my
boy! If you're alive, you can replace all of it, all of
what is being destroyed here!"

All I could mumble was, "Never again. Not for
this world of cruelty."

I stumbled out into the smoking streets in a state
of shock and confusion. The entire building was
falling down by then with a great crash.

Having been instilled by my mother with the idea
that family was a basic concept of living, I realized
with a start that I had to get to Brussels to find my
sister. The whole city of Antwerp was in turmoil, and
when I reached Brussels an hour later, I found the
same chaos everywhere. On the street, I ran into one
of the older diamond dealers, who was somehow related to my English-language pupil and who had

given me, on and off, some means of income at the
beginning of my stay there. He looked harried and,
after embracing my shoulders, leaned close to me and
handed me something. "This is most important," he
said. "I have great trust in you. I want you to hang
this little pouch around your neck. It contains the
address of my son. Please try to get it to him."

I hung the pouch around my neck. "Of course,
but I have to find my sister first. She may have rushed
to Antwerp to find *me*."

We parted. I didn't see him again for a very long
time.

MY SISTER WASN'T AT HOME, but a neighbor, a
scrawny old man who seemed to be trembling the
whole time we spoke, told me that she and her husband had moved toward the western coast, away
from the approaching German army. I made it my
own direction, to try to find them. The streets were
filled with people dragging valises and bags, and the
nervous noises of so many screaming for each other.
We all climbed aboard anything that was moving—
cars, trucks, any vehicle we could find—or hung off
the side of one. The desperation in every person's

eyes was unavoidable, unmistakable.

A day later, as part of this human stream, I had reached a border crossing into France—a road barrier that had been opened up manned by military people hanging around in blue-gray uniforms, but nobody could do anything. The only important thing was that you could speak French; if you did, there was no problem crossing over. I heard of some refugee camps in which people had been dragged out and killed on the assumption that they were spies for the invading German forces.

The German invasion of Belgium on May 10, 1940, marked the end of illusions. Europe finally had realized that it wasn't only "the Jews" who were at risk—everyone was fair game, unless of course you were among those people who had been waiting for the arrival of the Führer. People rushed here, there, aimlessly . . . until total chaos ensued. Trembling and fear hung in the air: Would the fabled Maginot line, that was to shield France from the Luftwaffe and the Wehrmacht, hold?

By June 25, that too had become a failed dream.

Chapter 10

I CONSTANTLY SCOURED MY SURROUNDINGS in the hope that, by chance, I would be able to spot my sister, but I couldn't. It wasn't summery yet, still late spring, though I saw no flowers—everything was so drab, overwhelmed by hordes of people moving in no discernable direction, confused, anxiety ridden, their familiar lives shattered, and in varying capacities to cope with this new reality. I passed French, English, and German troops also moving in utter confusion.

Not too far away to the west stretched the Straits of Dover—separating me from England—on the shores of which lay a place I had never heard of before called Dunkirk.

Resistance against the approaching Wehrmacht had completely collapsed; I fell into step with the British, who had abandoned everything and were fleeing into the harbor of the town. It was an ordinary waterfront; I followed what they were doing and ended up standing with them in water up to my neck.

Not much later, the Stukas came strafing in, and bombs and machine gun fire from above began to turn the water red with blood. From the other side of the Channel, the sky turned red too, followed by explosions and the acrid smell of gunpowder and burning flesh.

I REMAINED THERE IN THE water with the survivors for three entire days and nights, among the floating wounded and dead around me. I was overcome by a feeling of brotherhood for these soldiers in their impossible, fatal situation marked by futile gestures like trying to cover their heads with their arms to protect themselves against high-caliber ammunition. I was naturally in the same position that they were. I wanted somehow to be of use to them, to stand in solidarity with them, but I knew no English and so could not speak to a soul.

Little rowboats and motor launches kept crossing the Channel to pick up those who were still alive and climbed into them. These vessels, of course, were themselves not much safer; they were unsheltered targets for the machine gunners in the planes, who kept up a steady fire and killed many more. Still, in the mass hysteria of trying to avoid one certain death in the hope of chancing another, I struggled to join them.

When I was close by one of the boats, however, they pushed me away, shouting at me to keep off, that I wasn't a British soldier—until one, who looked like a teenager in a British uniform, finally said to me, in French, "I'm a Canadian. I can only tell you this— there's no chance for you to cross this way. Come with me. We'll try to get to Calais."

He actually guided me with some know-how— where he had acquired it, I have no idea. We practically crawled our way there, through all kinds of obstacles, debris piled high, destruction of buildings and obliterated roads, past more people dragging sacks filled with their possessions, more loud screaming as all manner of souls tried to find their families amid the endless, ongoing rain of explosives from the air and the diving fighter planes strafing the roads, their rounds kicking up explosions of dust and flying plaster, causing even greater panic and death.

Day turned to night; my companion and I kept moving, faster than anyone else because we were young and unburdened by any possessions to slow us down.

EARLY THE NEXT MORNING, WE reached Calais, which we barely touched, crawling our way along the waterfront. By then, the Canadian was talking to me as if we had known each other for a long time, and I felt a certain security in this.

He immediately disappeared onto one of the British troop ships lying there at anchor and soon reappeared and waved me closer. From the railing, he shook his head, shrugged sympathetically, and called out, "*No civilians!*"

They were eager to save their own people. I can't say I resented it at the time, but I knew I was on my own again, adrift once more.

So I crept back to the harbor. There was a small

building with a creaking sign crowning the entrance to an inn of sorts. As I entered, I saw a large counter crowded by one Frenchman on top of the next discussing the situation in loud, contradictory voices. It was impossible to get close.

I spotted a low door in the corner of the room. Giving up any hope of some other approach past the crowd to get something to eat, I opened it and found a staircase going down into the cellar.

In the dim light at the bottom of the stairs, I could make out a domed niche. I sank into a corner that gave me a little feeling of huddling in safety, and thoughts of anything disappeared as I fell into a deep sleep for the first time in ten days. I hadn't eaten in all that time, either. My energies—which were, after all, prodigious at nearly eighteen—had been thoroughly sucked out of me in the seawater, and the crawling and rushing.

This sleep revived me, like a plunge into a total refuge. The brain said nothing. All I felt was that fragile element of safety, huddled into that corner in the semi-darkness.

I don't know how much later, an enormous noise woke me. I still felt hindered, though, and when I was finally able to open my eyes, I was startled to see the daytime sky instead of the ceiling, and realized I was imprisoned in the rubble of the building—sheltered, really, by a fragment of the dome, which must have saved my life.

I couldn't move, though: I was buried amid the bricks and dust and fragments of wood. Oddly, though, I didn't panic. I invested all my energies instead in struggling to free myself from that interment, trying to gain some movement of my limbs, clawing at the bricks, every shift causing pain in my body here or there—from shoulder to chest to hip to knee—and making the effort an ordeal, a seemingly unending chore.

I kept at it, though, and finally disengaged my arms and legs after many, many hours of struggle. Had I been a little further away from the enclosed space I had fallen into the night before, I realized, I could not have survived. This thought energized me; it enabled me to journey beyond exhaustion, beyond pain, in the effort to live. I started climbing up through a huge mound of debris in front of me as if I were emerging from the bottom of a chasm, every movement again in pain, but I had to reach freedom.

Many more hours later, I was fighting my way past rats, which seemed to be somehow disturbed by my presence, zooming past me as I crawled. (Thus began an intimate, recurring engagement with rats that continued more or less unabated until the end of the war.) More horrifying still was to unexpectedly touch parts of shattered human bodies, a hand or a face—and *only* a face, with no head behind it—that suddenly appeared before me as I swept debris aside in my climb, and that should have driven me out of my mind but for the pulse of life that was so animating me.

I finally found a bottle of wine, apparently from the bar counter I couldn't get close enough to the previous day. I assembled a little pile of dust, dribbled some of the wine into it, and licked up the result. The wine did not help much assuage the hunger that was driving me nearly dizzy, though maybe it worked like a pain killer, because the aches all over my body seemed to diminish.

AT LAST, LIKE A MOUNTAIN climber, I made it to the top of that hill of rubble. I looked around in the bright sunshine. The entire vista before me was utterly silent. I was considering what to do next, sucking some energy from the sun beating down on me, when I heard a voice cry out, *"Hey, you! Frankse!"*

I turned and saw a squad of German-uniformed men at one end of the ruined street. I hollered back, *"You can speak German!"*

They marched up to me. "You a *deserter?"* the officer who had spoken to me asked.

I realized the trap I was in. I had to find some plausible explanation of my presence. "I—I am from Alsace-Lorraine," I told him. "We speak German there. I am no deserter. I've never *been* in the army. I'm strictly a civilian."

His smooth-shaven face cracked into a half-grin, and his blue eyes began to brighten as he pointed at me. "Then you're exactly what we need!" he shouted. "Come here!"

I said, "Yes, yes! Help me down, though, and I'll need something to eat before I can do anything for you."

They were happy to oblige, stuffing me full of food I could hardly recognize except that it *was* food . . .and it was heavenly. I had no idea what the future would hold for me, but I had the sense as I ate my way through what lay on the metal plate that it was solid food, real food after days and days of starvation.

And I felt, as Winston Churchill put it, that it was not the end of my struggle, or even the beginning of the end, but perhaps the end of the beginning—that maybe I would not die there and then, but begin my journey toward the rest of my life.

If you have time to live, your ears will blend the horrible noise of exploding ammunition, the crashes, the human screams; your eyes will, over time, dim the dancing of the fire on the waves. But nothing will ever help you forget the smell of that Dantean hell— the acrid, biting, nauseating stench. It will always be there to remind you of what you have escaped.

Part Two

THE CLOSING FIST

Chapter 11

T HEY GAVE ME A GERMAN uniform jacket and a little desk in the open air in a niche-like setup, and, after more ample food—cold sliced salami piled high on two slices of bread, and water—they marched a line of prisoners of war past me. I had to take down names, battalion numbers, and whatever identification each of them possessed. Some of them were still in uniform, some in civilian clothing; all were men, heads down, exhausted, completely defeated. On and off, I heard a British accent sneaking in among the French words: I immediately dismissed them as French prisoners, since I knew they would get a better shake that way.

This went on for four days in a row. I examined at all times my shoulder, my hip, my neck, urging myself to quick recuperation. They fed me regularly, and I slept on the ground.

By then, I was feeling myself again. I had for some time had my eye on a German bicycle that looked very attractive and very strong, and, as the last night fell, instead of huddling down to sleep once more on the hard ground, I made a little detour, grabbed the bicycle, and took off north, back to Brussels.

It was by then late summer, the countryside completely quiet, abandoned. There was no harvest, nothing. As soon as I got past the German checkpoints, I got rid of my German jacket and concentrated strictly on peddling.

The ride took me three days; I slept very little, just enough to keep myself awake, crouching in a little shelter here and there, huddling with my knees drawn up to my chest, in an alert position, ready to run at a moment's notice. I'd had enough food with the Germans to keep me going for some time.

I finally pedaled into Brussels and found my sister

and her husband in their old apartment. They hadn't gotten too far toward the border crossing into France after the occupation, and had returned in order to trace the status of their visa. They didn't look like refugees but more like all the other Belgians who had been adapting to the changed situation they were all in. I thought for a moment that they had come back to find out what had happened to me, but this was not the case. "It's been difficult for us," she said, though they hadn't had it as difficult as I had.

When I entered the bathroom to take a bath, I found the pouch the old diamond dealer had given me, which I had never opened, still hanging around my neck. After I had cleaned myself up and had a shave, I immediately began to search for him, since he had entrusted it to me for his son, whom I had never run into.

He was somehow still alive and in the diamond district, where I found him standing on the street, wearing a dilapidated suit and a wrinkled tie. I waved to him. He was shocked to see me and, when I gave him back the pouch, shook his head in disbelief. "I—"

"No, no," I said. "Don't say thank you. You

don't have to."

"I wasn't going to *thank* you," he replied. "I was just going to say, 'Stupid.' All you had to tell me you lost it. Let me show you what you have in that bag." He opened the pouch. It was packed with large diamonds, already cut and polished, tens of thousands of francs' worth, though I had no way to judge—a fortune, certainly.

I just mumbled, "So glad I didn't lose it."

In the meantime, I was approached by another former refugee who knew I had studied at the Academie, had had a bit of architectural training, and said, "We could get a job, you know, preparing recreation facilities for German officers." He was in his early thirties, somewhat neglectful of his appearance but very enthusiastic with regard to this project.

"Okay," I said. "Sounds like a good idea to *me*."

We went to two buildings that had been confiscated by the German authorities to see if we could find someone with whom we could discuss how to make the buildings comfortable.

We spoke to a few officers—I didn't know what their positions were, but I gathered that they were somehow responsible for the facility. They were stony-faced, athletically built men, but they soon proved to be not very efficient. When they found out I was fluent in French and Flemish, one of them proposed that I travel to Paris with some of the officers to hire women for "entertainment purposes"—they didn't trust the Belgian woman with their families so close.

We found four other refugees who were to be our "executives" in this venture—to work out the details of the ideas and plans we devised, take care of the bookkeeping (though this was not a precise endeavor by any means), and so on.

In the meantime, my sister was becoming a nervous wreck, having realized it was impossible to get permission to travel through occupied France to Portugal, where her visa was waiting for her in Lisbon. At one encounter with my elderly diamond dealer, he insisted I tell him why I seemed so preoccupied. When I explained my sister's predicament, he said, "For your sake, I'll try my best to find a solution for her and her husband. Come see me tomorrow."

THE FOLLOWING DAY, HE SAID, "Listen carefully. I know a group of diamond dealers who are invested in Cuban tobacco farms. I was able to get an agreement from the Cuban consulate to give your sister two visas to Cuba, with the secret understanding that they will never land in Cuba but just use the documents as a special transportation permit through German-occupied France to take a boat from Lisbon."

I was overwhelmed by this kindness, but then my sister came back to tell me that they knew two other couples in the same position as they were, and asked if they could somehow be included in this generous offer.

I asked my friend. He replied, "Typical Jewish thinking, I must say. . . you give somebody a finger, and they want the whole arm! But let me see."

He did, and the two couples were also granted these visas.

I went to the Customs office in Brussels and was able, with Flemish friendship, to acquire all kinds of steamer trunks for the six travelers. With the visas, they also received the necessary travel permits from the German authorities and were soon set to go. It took about ten days to get their travel arrangements together.

My sister asked me, "Why don't you come with

us? Portugal might be a door to freedom for you."

But at that moment, an image swept over me of my parents. It blossomed in my head. When I told her I might prefer to go back to Vienna and try to stay with them to find a solution of their predica-

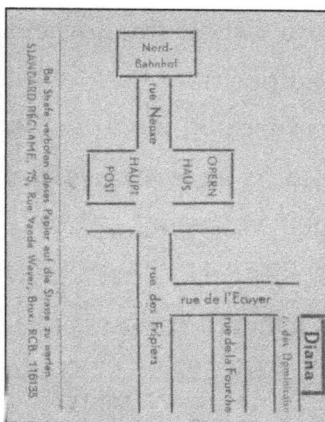

Front and back of the advertising card for Diana, the German officers' club I designed in Brussels in 1940

ment, what future steps might be taken to get them out as well, she told me she thought it was no more than a foolish notion.

My co-workers agreed; one told me, "But you will only become a burden to them and not benefit them whatsoever."

At one encounter with a stern-faced, austere general named von Falkenhorst, who came to visit the officers' facilities, however, he—having learned I was still registered as a student at the Academie—asked me if there was anything he could do to repay our design efforts on behalf of the Wehrmacht. His uniform had the necessary red rank marks, and he wore an Iron Cross, though, despite his forbidding posture and position, he was a decent enough, cordial fellow and treated me in an almost fatherly way. "Well," I said, "I have always been very impressed by the Munich Museum. . . ."

"Indeed!" he said with satisfaction. "All right. Whenever you're ready, come to me, and I'll arrange a *laisser passer* to Munich for you."

Chapter 12

I N SPITE OF ALL THE efforts people were making to convince me that it was a foolish thing to attempt to be of help to my parents, that I would more likely become a burden to them, that I had to be realistic and come to terms with the fact that there would be no exit from the clutches of the Nazis, I resolved to go to Vienna. I didn't even try to engage in speculating that generalizations about future events did not necessarily predict the outcome of any single case one faced. For me, there was no other way—I couldn't have lived with myself letting them die without even attempting to help. In that sense, it was a selfish decision: I was actually looking out, as my American brethren now say, for number one.

I went to the Kommandatur the next day, which was housed in an older Baroque stone building that the German command had taken over. It was a busy place, with uniformed men running back and forth, moving about importantly, sheaves of papers in their hands or under their arms.

When my arrival was announced, General von Falkenhorst himself appeared in the reception area, dressed as usual in a perfectly pressed gray uniform with lots of medals and indications of rank. He handed me an oblong piece of cardboard, smiled in his faint way, and said, "This is all you will need. I hope you enjoy Munich and the artwork sheltered there! Good luck to you!" He took both my shoulders and added, "Enjoy it to the fullest! You deserve it!" He had, obviously, no idea, not the remotest suspicion, that I was a Jew.

I packed up my few things, including my shaving set from the three girls, in a sack, taking it for granted that I was disappearing from the surface of the Earth; though I was sorry to know that the chance of survival for all of my friends and co-workers in Brussels was very remote indeed, I knew it was hardly worse than my own.

I left for the train station. The Gare de Nord (a very unprepossessing place more like a supermarket than the dark, smoky places favored by film makers to drive up the suspense), clean and efficient, was not especially busy that morning. There was, of course, a certain degree of activity and movement, people hurrying to their trains or, glancing at their wrist watches, waiting for friends and relatives to arrive.

I had enough German marks in my pocket that I had accumulated, in trading for materials for the creation of the nightclub and attending facilities, to pay for my ticket to Munich. I also had the francs that the diamond dealer had given me (so long ago, it seemed), saying, "Soon, soon you will earn it!"

The train was a great excitement for me. I tucked myself into the corner of a cabin and went to sleep almost immediately.

I was interrupted a few times by conductors and border guards when we crossed into Germany, where the *laisser passer* worked perfectly, without any difficulties whatsoever, no questions asked. (I had my *carte d'identité* too, which identified me as a Belgian resident—there had been no religious or racial factors listed at the time I acquired it, by contrast with German passports, which bore an prominent "J" for Jews—but no one asked to see it.)

ABOUT TEN HOURS LATER, A somewhat crackly loudspeaker announced that we were arriving in Munich. I made it my business to oversleep, so that, when the conductor—a big, elderly guy in a navy uniform, with a very elegant white handlebar moustache—found me on the way to Vienna and said, "You forgot to get off in Munich. Why don't you get off at the next stop, and I'll give you a return ticket to Munich?" I replied,

"Well, maybe on my way back. I might as well continue to Vienna for now. I have some business there, too."

I paid him for another ticket and was again traveling without difficulties. I went back to what looked like sleep, as always the best safe haven for me—eyes closed, breathing regularly, paying no attention to people coming on or getting off but attentive to the possibility of any noise that didn't fit, any incongruity that might hint of danger. But this instinct had, by then, I must reiterate, *become* an instinct, not a conscious effort. Too many months had already passed for me to require conscious thought when my survival was at stake. Almost everything I did was second nature: maybe that was why it drew so little attention to me, and I became more or less invisible, a wraith of smoke.

More hours went by.

FINALLY, IN THE EARLY MORNING hours, we pulled into the Westbanhof station in Vienna. It was a cloudy day at the end of 1940 or the very beginning of '41, the sun fighting a losing battle to appear. I slipped off the train, left the station, and found a taxi. I gave the driver the address. He was either a Czech or Hungarian and had more than enough difficulty even understanding where I was asking him to take me, much less the ability or willingness to engage in the aimless chatter taxi drivers are prone to the world over.

Close to half an hour later, I told him to let me off a few blocks from my parents' apartment, and familiarized myself again with all the details of the neighborhood—sidewalks, stores, and building entrances. I hadn't seen them in three years, but they had changed very little, at least on the outside.

I entered the building, hurried up to the second floor, and rang the bell. I waited until I recognized the little woman who opened the door as my mother. I had somehow in the intervening years outgrown her. I bent down to embrace her and lifted her off the ground. We had an unusual relationship that way—I had never done such a thing to her, only to girlfriends.

She kept staring at me with big eyes and finally asked, "How are you, Kurt?"

"Fine, Mama. I'm fine!"

A long pause followed. "What. . .why are you here now?" she finally continued. "Why have you come?"

"We have to be together," I told her. "My idea of family is a *union*."

By then, my father was standing behind her, taking in every word. He shook my hand in his formal, emotionally ungiving way.

The apartment, I immediately noticed, had been broken up into smaller accommodations; my parents were occupying only one little bedroom. Three other families were sharing the remaining space.

We went into the bedroom and sat down. "We

applied for an American visa," she told me, "but they refused me for health reasons, because I have diverticulitis."

I was very upset by this, outraged that the United States would have such a reason for denying people a visa at such a time, when they were facing such risks, such potential calamities. (I went with them to the U. S. consulate and had lengthy discussions about this. The consular officials eventually admitted that the denial had been a misunderstanding, and that they would see to it that the application process would proceed. On July 4, of all days, my parents were told they in fact could come to pick up their visa.)

The three of us shared our one room with another Jewish couple, complete strangers who had lost their apartment too, all five of us sleeping in that small space and arranging some system for organizing clothing and such, and for using the bathroom. It was, of course, extraordinarily awkward and uncomfortable.

I HAD TO PRESENT MYSELF for obligatory labor as part of my residence in Vienna. I went to an office somewhere in the First District of the city, housed in a compound of small buildings one section of which was staffed by young Jewish men.

"I need to present myself," I told one of them, and was soon directed to an address where I ended up carrying a piano, with two elderly people, from the fifth floor of a house down the stairs to the street. The office was responsible for confiscating the contents of apartments whose Jewish inhabitants had been relocated.

I soon learned that an SS officer named Witke was in charge of the whole operation. He had a face that could have been carved from marble and had no human expression whatsoever, and he spoke in short barks. He wore rimless glasses, and his uniform cap set squarely over short-cut, sandy blond hair. When I passed him a few times in the halls of the office, it seemed to me he had registered who I was in some dim but precise, feral way.

The streets were devoid of human sparkle. We used to go to a coffeehouse and sit in front of one cup of coffee, reading all the newspapers, with their wooden hanger dowels securely in place, for hours on end. It was pretty depressing, and more depressing still was the constant concern over what would happen to us, what the Nazis had in mind—deportation, we understood, not to concentration camps (we had heard about one of those, which had been opened for inspection by Western nations and at which concerts and lectures were offered, though we knew nothing of the horrors of Auschwitz and Buchenwald), but to small centers in rural Poland. In any case, I felt more than ever (perhaps because I was so inactive) that I was living on borrowed time.

WITHIN WEEKS, A MAN I vaguely recognized stopped me in the street and said, "Didn't you go to school with my son? Aren't you the one who always drew all kinds of cartoons?"

He was rather young-looking, handsome, the father of two sons, one of whom had emigrated to South Africa. Where my old school chum was, I didn't quite get, though he must have been somewhere with family in the countryside. The father was Lutheran, though his wife may have been Jewish.

"...Why, yes," I said.

"Have you acquired in the interim perhaps some knowledge of the restoration of paintings?"

I said, "Just a very little bit, superficially."

"Maybe," he replied, "this might be of help anyway. I'd like you to come with me to the Museum of Fine Arts."

It was a pretty imposing place, across from the Natural History Museum and separated from it by an enormous statue of the Empress Maria Teresa in a voluminous dress.

The interview that followed once we got to the museum was very unfriendly. The father introduced me to a fully bearded gentleman in a white smock. "Yes," this martinet said to me in an imperious voice, "we are in great need of qualified people to replace some of the ones who have been inducted and are now in Russia. But we cannot take chances, so if you want, we can let you work on some projects and judge you by the results."

As a test, he had me restore certain discrete areas of various canvases.

By accident, as we were leaving, one of the bureaucratic assistants was with me. Suddenly, uniformed men appeared and stopped us. "*You!*" one of them snapped. "Why aren't you working?"

I looked up, stunned. It was Witke.

". . .And, by the way, where's your star?"

"Oh. Here," I said, opening my briefcase. "I didn't mean to hide it."

The man I was with said, "Wait a second—this young man may be a gift from heaven. We don't know yet."

The Sturmbahnführer absorbed this information stolidly before he declared, "Tomorrow morning, in my office!"

WHEN I GOT THERE THE next day, he leapt up from his desk and shouted, "Why didn't you *tell* me you have these skills? No more dragging heavy weights for you! From now on, you will get first inspection of any apartment that is being taken over, and you will pick the paintings that are worthwhile and have them moved to your apartment. And then you can do the work that is needed on them."

". . .But, Sturmbahnführer, I have no *room*. We're sharing an apartment with three other families."

He offered me his version of a smile; it reminded me of a snake's mouth just before it is about to strike. "No problem," he assured me. "Let me double-check, but stay a moment." He picked up the telephone and, when he had finished making the call, gave me an address and said, "Go there, and see if it is appropriate."

IT WAS A FIVE-ROOM APARTMENT, huge, on the fifth floor of a building on the Tabor Strasse, a main street in the Second District. My parents and I immediately moved into this paradise, which was twice the size of the one we had been living in. (Many acquaintances who needed temporary shelter took advantage of the

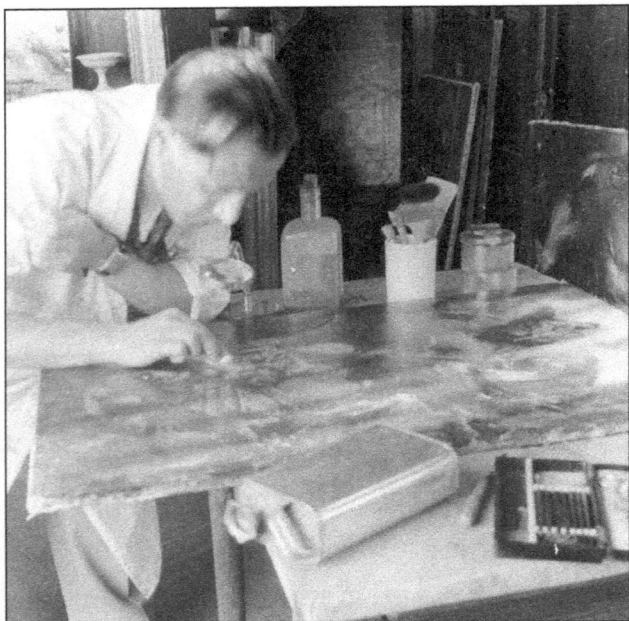

Restoring a 15th-century canvas, Museum of Fine Arts, Vienna, 1940–1941

Restoring a Quinten Massys canvas of 1550,
Museum of Fine Arts, Vienna, 1940–1941

place as time went on.)

I started collecting artworks from the homes of those who had been deported—Impressionists, old master drawings, whatever I could find, including the modern work that was very popular among the Viennese. I suspected that this was a side business for Witke.

Life looked promising for me and my parents at

that point, even with all the goings on. (Mainly, as I have said, the deportations were being explained at the time as resettlements of people with trades who could establish new cities in the countryside. The purpose was to cleanse the Aryan inhabitants of their Jewish contaminants. This was still early in 1941— the concentration camps would become a fact only later—so the deportations could proceed calmly.)

We also had a telephone in the apartment, so I gave my mother a phone number where she could reach me in case of an imminent catastrophe.

I pedaled between our apartment and the museum, and from one confiscated apartment to the next, daily, carefully hiding the yellow star because the museum would probably not have agreed to have me working there if they had known who I really was—a half-hour or hour here or there, on the run constantly, trying to see if I could actually manage to do the restorations. My training in Antwerp had been theoretical, abstract—it was like trying to do something by reading a textbook on the subject.

I also seemed to be a desirable target for young ladies then. Probably there weren't enough men around. I met them everywhere—at the museum, in the streets, in the vicinity of the apartments I was evaluating; Viennese are outgoing people, friendly as Americans in many ways.

Then I got a phone call from my mother with a one-word message: "Come."

Chapter 13

I HURRIED BACK. THE MESSAGE I found when I got there, hurriedly scrawled on a piece of paper, read: *Will be at doctor around the corner.* It was still possible at those early months of 1941 for a Jewish doctor to keep his office open in Vienna.

She had run to him, barefoot, in her nightgown. One of our friends, who had slept over, had apparently been followed by the secret police, since he was a refugee escaping deportation; fortunately, my mother had not been held responsible for his presence, though the friend was taken away. She was, nevertheless, so terrified that she had fled to the doctor, who had calmed her.

From that moment to today, seventy years later, a ringing telephone has in some dark recess of my soul remained a portent of unpleasant news for me, however much I know better.

When I got to the doctor, who was named Troller—an elderly man in a crumpled white coat, with a worried face, who looked a lot like my father—she had already calmed down. "She'll be all right. Keep her away from problems," he whispered to me.

This close encounter with disaster had only occurred because we were harboring refugees under our roof. I found it difficult to refuse temporary shelter to people anyway. It was very dangerous, though— we risked always losing our stability, maybe even winding up being deported ourselves.

Not long after that incident, the Jewish secretary to Witke, who was also a friend of mine, brought me a message: Witke had received approval from Gestapo headquarters in Vienna to acquire a special permit that would guarantee me and one additional person security from deportation because of my positive contribution to his efforts .

The secretary, who had probably just completed his training in law school but knew enough to run the Sturmbahnführer's office, explained this to the three of us in the living room of our apartment. It was good news, but it presented me with a profound problem: I would be able to protect only my father or my mother.

Minutes later, I found my father hunting for papers. "What are you doing?" I asked him.

"I will present myself to assure your mother's safety, and yours."

"No way!" I told him. "I have come back all this distance in order to be together with you and live the best way we can, and if need be, to die together if the time should come. *No exceptions.*"

This came as something of a shock to him. I had never before spoken to my father in that way. I figured I would have to find a better solution than the one Witke was offering.

I soon connected with people who would be able to smuggle us across the border into Yugoslavia. They were friends of the father of my old schoolmate who had referred me to the museum in the first place.

I went to see them—a group of working people

who dealt in moving merchandise from one place to another. They bought tickets for the three of us to Bucharest, the farthest destination on that line. Yugoslavia was the closest border to Vienna, and my fantasy was that, should we reach Bucharest, I might be a desirable employee to the museum there—if there was one. There were no more Jews in Yugoslavia either; it was empty, and the effort to find more had ceased. I suspected that, if we could remain unnoticed, we might slip by. My mother was fifty-six years old at the time; my father must have been around sixty.

WE PACKED UP A FEW bundles and left that lovely apartment very early on a morning in June. We were smuggled out of the country with our tickets in our pockets, to avoid any complications at the Yugoslav border.

Right across the border from Austria, we boarded the train, but not too long afterwards it was stopped for inspection. The local Yugoslav police soon came down the compartments asking for papers. They were dressed in uniforms very close to the German military standard, and barked orders. When I presented my identity card from Belgium, it seemed to be sufficient, and the explanation I gave them, that the elderly people with me were my servants, somehow also passed muster with the policeman, who moved on to the next compartment.

IT WAS A VERY LENGTHY trip, nearly two days; there were inspections every so often, but we managed to complete the journey, in time crossing the border again into Romania.

Some acquaintances of my parents were our first stop in Bucharest—an older couple, retirees—and, following their advice, we went to present ourselves at the local police station. (They should have advised us to find a lawyer instead, who might have prevented what happened next and enabled us to escape deportation.)

Lack of communication—we had no common language with the uniformed policemen, who spoke to us an abrupt tongue in a small, run-down building in the middle of the city—made it difficult to express ourselves, but they eventually guided us to a prison cell rather than register us. They fed us simple food— a yellow paste that they called *mamaliga* and that was a substitute for bread, and some cheese.

We lingered there for two days. We were debating with some of the guards the reason why we were being held, and in time came to understand that Jews were not desirable in Romania. Something, we were told, would have to be done with us. I still believed that the few photographs I had from the Vienna Museum would open the doors for me. Finally, they informed us that our next stop would be Cernowitz in the Bucovina, a province in northern Romania.

I told myself that that would probably be as good a place as any.

ANOTHER LENGTHY TRAIN TRIP FOLLOWED. We left the station after we reached our destination and found a great assembly of people, visibly Jewish families, local people who spoke German with a Romanian accent, and we finally got an explanation of our position: The new laws and regulations were following German rules—to deport as many Jews as possible to the Ukraine, to clean Romania, as Germany had planned all along. Meanwhile, the locals were seizing possessions from the newcomers' baggage. I called out to some of the younger people to surround the older ones and chase these thieves away.

Soon, we were loaded into another train and shipped to Mogilev, the capital of the Ukraine. The trip lasted about eight hours. Realizing that we would be separated into small groups once we disembarked, I found an escape close to the border of the town and, in my inexperienced way, figured that, if we could separate from the others and try to find a shelter for ourselves, we would be better off. I found out, however, that the others had all kinds of possessions—coins, silver, gold, and such sewn into the linings of their clothes. We could not compete with any of them. We had come totally unprepared.

I found a roadway with a ditch that was sufficient to hide ourselves in, with views of small ruins of buildings. For the moment, it was the best place we could manage. We could not, then, begin to comprehend what our situation would become, and how difficult it would be to survive. It was late summer, and the evenings had started to grow cool. "I wish," my mother picturesquely sighed, as women are inclined to do, "I had my fur coat."

On June 22, 1941, Germany annexed Romania; a day later, that annexation was complete. Romania had already ceded territory to Hungary and Bulgaria—to become a German satellite was a foregone conclusion, since Russia (the only other alternative) was an ancient enemy. The persecution of Jews was still spotty at that moment: The Nazis were more interested in the benefits of slave labor.

The Axis powers were, however, unaware that the Soviet Union was preparing for all-out war although nominally an ally of Germany. The world as a whole ought to have anticipated that these two totalitarian giants, each hungry to conquer all the world, would eventually lock horns. During these years, both were jockeying for power over their neighbors. All of Europe remained in turmoil. For Jews, the deadly game of hide-and-seek escalated, with Underground forces beginning to organize.

Chapter 14

HAD TO SEE HOW I could provide food in such a situation. To buy from local peasants was impossible—we lacked the means. Other, more far-sighted (or lucky) people had sewn their meager wealth into the linings of their clothes before departing. We had had none of these things to begin with, and no opportunity to take advantage of them even if we had.

I wanted, though, to avoid becoming part of a group that would be shipped from one camp to another, heavily penalized and uncertain of any future steps (particularly because I had my parents to think of, which meant the sorts of dodges I had invented earlier would no longer be feasible). That much I understood in my gut.

In the course of this inner struggle, this search for a way to survive, I met a young man who had come from Cernovitz and who spoke all the languages of the region—German, Romanian, Rutanian, Yiddish, and Russian. He discovered us on the roadside by the ditch where we were sleeping. He had a boyish appearance—he was about a foot shorter than I was and looked like one of my schoolmates, brown-haired, brown-eyed, and slender (there were no fat people in those days, since everybody was starving, but his thinness was particularly pronounced), and he had traces of a dark beard on his face. "Where do you come from?" he called out, "and what language do you speak?"

"German," I called back. He understood me because that language was still being used by the Jewish population of Cernowitz, which had once been a part of the Austro-Hungarian Empire.

This graceful creature considered himself a true helper of others. I wanted him, first of all, to help me learn Yiddish—in case we *were* absorbed by some group, it would be difficult for me to communicate in German with people who spoke various other tongues, and German was, moreover, the language of the oppressors. I figured Yiddish would be a near equivalent of Dutch or Flemish, which I had learned quickly, tracing the German roots of almost every word, when I entered the Academie, since the teaching there had been in French and Flemish.

"Can you teach me Yiddish?" I said. "Can you? I hope it's not too difficult."

He said, with a bright smile, "Done! I will stand by you. My name is Freddie."

I embraced him. "You can call me Kurt," I said, and explained that the two older people I was with were my parents.

"Where can we find something to eat?" I asked. We had had no time to even concentrate on eating; we hadn't had a morsel, in any case, in a day or two.

I told my mother and father to wait for me, and Freddie swiftly guided me, under a gray sky threatening to rain, to a huge dump on the outskirts of town—not too far away, though you had to know the turns to take on the streets—where, he told me, it would be possible to find piles of raw potato peels deposited by the Germans to fatten the pigs for

Christmas.

When we got there, he warned me that, if the Germans caught us stealing from that dump, they would not hesitate to shoot us. I took a breath and nodded, as if to ask what choice we had.

We hurried into the place and grabbed potato peels as quickly as I could, opening my shirt and stuffing as many into it as would fit before hurrying back to the ditch.

"Here," I told my parents. "Now we have food to survive."

My mother looked as this repast with disgust written all over her face and exclaimed, "But it's *garbage!*"

I asked her to put a piece in her mouth anyway.

"Impossible," she declared.

"Listen!" I told her. "This is our only means of staying alive, Mama. Do you understand what I'm telling you? Our only means. We have to overcome every and any obstacle, any objection. We have to do that from now on. It will probably get worse than it is now."

Finally, she ate the raw peel, which I noticed foamed up in the mouth as I chewed it because of the starch meeting the saliva in my mouth. I had never tasted anything like it before. It was bitter and very unpleasant but nourishing. My father ate it without voicing complaints. "We have to respect this stuff," I told him.

I SPENT AS MUCH TIME as I could concentrating on Yiddish while we tried to keep warm. Fall came on, and the weather kept getting colder. At night, my father and I enveloped my mother with our bodies. I had meanwhile learned from Freddie of the existence of two campsites in Moghilev with perhaps one or two hundred people in each. His parents, he had told me, were in one of them.

Freddie became more and more of a true friend. I repeated the words that he taught me in Yiddish until I could speak them, and he did what he could to improve my accent and word choices. All this took place in that ditch by the side of the road. He disappeared as night fell, and we tried to sleep—to put our *minds* to sleep, that is. Hopefully, we would not become involved in any of the procedures being imposed on other deportees by the German and Romanian authorities.

The stories that Freddie told were not very encouraging. Groups were exploited, sometimes starved, and moved further into Russia. The plan was to eliminate the Jews from the region. My thoughts remained, nevertheless, somewhat hopeful for the immediate future—elements like hunger, cold weather, and rain and snow could be overwhelming and impossible to cope with, but I believed that, if I could provide for my mother and father and not abandon hope, we would make it through. I had that conviction; I can't honestly say how I managed to have it—there was very little to encourage such thinking—but I did.

MANY DAYS PASSED. IT GOT colder and colder, and my dependence on Freddie grew greater and greater. I could see, in the distance, the outline of a totally destroyed building on the horizon; it housed a pack of wolves that howled at the moon each night. It was a ghostly experience, indelible, more than a photograph in the mind, more like a symbol of our return to an arboreal world more than half wild in which our forebears had lived thousands of years before.

One day, as we were creeping back from a sortie

after food, I was walking backwards in consternation over a complicated Yiddish phrase when all of a sudden, I felt I had stumbled into something behind me. I turned around and saw a stout man in a blue-green uniform, thankfully not German but Romanian. He had a big, round face with eyes almost crawling out of it, and a big mouth spitting hard words in Romanian at me: "In your mother's vagina! Devil take you! What are you *grinning* at?" These words came at me like machine-gun fire, and he pulled his gun out of its holster and pressed it against my temple.

I didn't understand a word of this, but the fact that I could see his willingness to shoot made me stagger backwards.

At that moment, little Freddie stepped between us and said, "Please, Lieutenant, forgive him! He doesn't understand a word of our language. He just came here from Vienna."

The response was quick. The officer reholstered the weapon and exclaimed, "*What?* Why, this is a *miracle!* My mother was traveling and gave birth to me in Vienna, and since I was a sickly baby, we remained there for some time. I learned to absorb and to look and try to understand, and I don't know how much. . .but I reached the understanding that Vienna was inhabited by *leather experts*."

As Freddie finished translating, the lieutenant pointed at me, and said, "Are *you* a leather expert?"

"Absolutely," Freddie told him.

"My name is Codoş," said the stout man, an enormous grin spreading across his features. "Listen to me, my leather expert. We will have a truck leaving for Romania soon. There's a small town there that has three leather factories working for the Romanian and German armed forces. They need leather experts, and my contribution to them will bring me a medal of honor! *You* will be on that truck!"

"But," I said, "I have my parents here. . . ."

"There's *plenty* of room on the truck," he said.

I wondered if I could get Freddie and his parents onto the truck, too. Soon enough, I had, though Freddie for some reason didn't come; there *was* a nice little group, however—all strangers to me—who did.

Chapter 15

A FTER HOURS OF TRAVEL, the truck—open to the elements, the late-fall weather chilling us all to the bone—pulled up in a small town called Bacau in the northern regions of Romania. It was something of a station for the German command in the region; however, the town was still inhabited by Jews who served the German authorities each in his or her own manner, which was extraordinary, really, in the waning months of 1942, when the Final Solution had been put into effect all over German-dominated Europe.

As we drove down the streets, the chilly wind

ripped the hat off my head and carried it away. I covered my head with my hands instead. But a young boy called out something from the street (I couldn't understand what he was saying), pulled off his own hat, a *căciulă*, and threw it up to me. It saved me from a bad cold at the very least—illness then, any sapping of one's health, was a doorway to death.

A profound friendship developed between me and him, a Jew whose father was the town photographer and whom he helped in a major capacity. (My influence on him began after the Russians liberated Romania, when he came to Vienna and started his studies there and got involved in all kinds of businesses, working, among other things, for a brokerage house in Germany and South America, learning Spanish and Portuguese. These young Romanians had an extensive network of associations that was almost worldwide. Much later, he became a customer of mine in the United States; I designed and built everything for him, and when he decided to move to Florida, he took every piece with him and still treasures it. . .but that's another story.)

We were soon disembarked from that truck. There was a Jewish committee of sorts there to welcome us, mainly to see that we had housing, and my parents and I were situated in a small house belonging to a Great War widow. Communication was strictly notional, since she spoke only Romanian, of which we knew not a word. She was a scrawny little soul who always had her shoulders pulled up to her ears.

But Mother somehow communicated with her in the special language women have of understanding one another, and, finally, got involved in cooking food that was way different from the raw potato peels upon which we had been subsisting for so long. She learned all kinds of Romanian recipes—like *mamaliga*, the cornmeal mush that occurs, in one version or another, over so much of Europe, and *castravete vinete*, "purple cucumber," an eggplant, purple onion, and egg dish with all kinds of things added to it. They make their own version of borscht too there, totally different from the one most other Europeans are familiar with. Meat sauces, mixed in enormous combinations with potatoes, also found their way to the table in the kitchen, or in our room (a third room served as the owner's).

Bathroom facilities were very simple—the toilet

was two footsteps and a hole; water consisted of an outdoor pump and was most refreshing to me, because I had to get out early for work at the leather factory—six o'clock every morning, *munca obsteasca* (Romanian for "obligatory labor") six days a week.

I WAS RECEIVED, LEATHER EXPERT *soi-disant*, the morning after we arrived, once I had climbed to the third floor of the factory. There were large tables there with already-tanned hides pinned to them in all kinds of ways and in patterns that were at first totally incomprehensible to me. They were supposed to be turned into boots for German officers, I learned from one of the workers, a tall man in his late thirties or early forties with an unshaven face and a hank of light-brown hair over his forehead.

I stood there like a tree, not knowing what to do, and stammered in Yiddish, "Can you help me, show me what to do, how to do whatever I need to?"

"Sorry," he said. "I have to produce. I have no time. I can't give you any."

It didn't take long for the director of the plant, a very strict person, big and clean-shaven, with dark hair, who seemed in my esteem to be, or act like, an older man, and who tried to effect a military manner, to tell me to leave the floor and go to a lower level.

The lower level consisted of long, dark rooms with low ceilings, one of which I was directed to. They had long benches with about thirty men seated next to each other, with other benches in front of them that they used as table surfaces. Their job was to take sewn leather parts and stretch them over wooden lasts. There were bowls filled with small nails, into which they reached, threw a handful of nails into their mouths, and spit out one at a time onto the shoe that had been stretched over the last, followed quickly by a stroke of a shoemaker's hammer. It went like machine-gun fire.

I figured I shouldn't have difficulty copying what they were doing at a slower pace, but it didn't take long for my fingers to start spurting blood all over the tabletop and the last sitting in front of me. My asking for help was totally misunderstood, and I realized that my abilities were totally inadequate to the task.

Again it did not take long for the supervisor of the floor, whom I cannot recall beyond the fact that he was an ugly-looking, impatient man, to say, "No good. *Down.* Go down to the next floor!"

So I descended even further in the hierarchy of factory skills.

All these leather-working facilities, I soon learned, had been built around a square inner court, in the middle of which sat a lake. Raw hides were delivered regularly by truck and unloaded into this lake, which was filled with a very strong-smelling liquid that I soon realized was tanning fluid.

I was directed down there by the supervisor, told to wade into the lake—which came up as far as my chest—fully clothed, to move around the hides that were soaking in it, and to check them to see how far the tanning process had advanced. I had no idea what that meant, but I did what they told me to do and tried to look as if I knew what they were talking about.

I discovered I wasn't alone—companies of rats were tumbling around in that lake, too. They hardly bothered me, however. When you have lived for a while on potato peels that you can get shot for stealing, you develop a different sense of the world's essential nature; the rats and I were both simply doing our collective best to get by. The only great discomfort I felt in the lake was the constant odor that surrounded me from the tanning fluid.

Soon, after the hours I spent there, I was surrounded by a whole group of young people trying to integrate me into the system. One was a schoolteacher, a handsome young man who said he would take time out to teach me Romanian. "It's important for communication with your superiors," he said.

The others proposed some sort of entertainment for the Sunday we had off—a more-or-less constant get-together with them, to whom I somehow appeared, I gathered, as if I had descended from the moon. I was more advanced in the dance-step repertoire than they were, which was a great attraction for them. The wind-weathered fedora that had blown off my head the day I first arrived, and which had in time been found and returned to me, became an object of great admiration, since it was a Borsalino, which made much more of an impression on them than it ever had on me.

As I milked my Dutch language skills for Yiddish, I started to give up portions of my French, and distant memories of Latin, for Romanian. I juggled around my language skills to the best of my inventiveness.

Most of the time, it worked. I could make myself understood—and, since I had always thought of languages as melodies, what I spoke usually sounded much better than it meant.

ONE DAY, A GERMAN INSPECTION group came to the factory and asked for certain boxes to be handed to them from the inventory shelves, which they planned to open in order to assess the quality of the helmet linings they contained. Naturally, they spoke German—and their response to the alien tongue of the management staff was pretty abrasive. The chief inspector growled in exasperation, "Find us someone who speaks *German,* you hear?"

The director started hunting around, and I was soon pulled out of my lake and presented to this chief of the inspection group, a uniformed Wehrmacht officer, broad-shouldered, tall, and statuesque. We had instant contact through my command of the language, as precise as they could have wished.

He listened to me in apparent satisfaction and concluded, "I'm very—*overly*—pleased! From now on, *you* will represent the factory when we appear. But what smells so *horrendous?*"

"...I'm, uh," I said, "part of the chemistry department, sir. I can't just—"

"Let them find somebody else to do that! I want you to take over the supervision of the helmet-lining department, effective immediately." He said so to the plant director too, and made sure he understood. I stood by, nonplussed to say the least, but I immediately knew the change would be a real improvement for me.

It was a very big change. I soon met the group of about twenty-five members of the department I had miraculously assumed control over, who had a rather suspicious attitude towards me because, since they were the slave laborers and the Germans were the exploiters, they naturally thought I was part of the second category—and my Romanian didn't completely erase that feeling.

Chapter 16

⌒⌒⌒

I HAD TO SET DOWN rules quickly in order to make the best use of the premium-quality lamb's wool at our disposal, which had been left on the skins. The department was a large hall in one of the wings of the factory. It had one wall with three double windows, an eight-foot ceiling, and wooden floors. It measured about twenty by forty feet, and all twenty-five of my workers men.

The process was simplicity itself. There was a machine to cut out the patterns with considerable economy, and another that stamped out grommets, through which cords would run to attach the linings to the helmets. "I don't know what you're thinking," I said once I had the entire staff assembled and alone with me. "Let me first of all tell you who I am. I'm like all of you—a refugee here, with a family, trying to stay alive. I got this job because I can speak German. That's it. Do you understand this, what I'm trying to tell you? I have only one goal here. My job is to keep all of us alive."

There were to be no shortcuts, I went on to explain, and I wanted high levels of production—not for the love of the Germans, but, as I explained, "So all of you can continue to work here instead of being deported. These people will not hesitate to get rid of us if we don't deliver what they expect. So we will. We will see to it that we do, that we satisfy them— and that we survive."

The ensuing silence was eventually broken by a series of grunts and the cautious nodding of heads illuminated by a light peculiarly soft and pearly that day. They seemed to be agreeing with me; they could, I was relieved to see, grasp the obvious. So began my adventure as the head of a department manufacturing war materiel for the Wehrmacht.

The pay was minuscule, but whenever my men

needed leather from any part of the factory, I simply stuck it under my shirt, and, since I was a foreman, nobody searched me when I left the floors. I could help them this way achieve a few more benefits, because we soon earned a reputation for consistently reaching our production goals. Little by little, this recognition from the other departments, and much more importantly from the German supervisors, gained the trust of those under me.

We worked from six to six every day except Sunday. Because of my rank, I was also off on Saturday. No food, needless to say, was ever provided for us by the factory. Each worker had to bring in his own—*mamaliga*, herring and onions, and a local sheep's cheese that was available and cheap. There was no bread. We ate simply but enough to keep us at work. It was late fall by then and devilishly cold, and the place unheated, so we all dressed as warmly as we could.

The workers had to stamp a lining out of skins—strips about six inches wide with one wavy border, so that, when the lining was drawn together, it would form a cap—clean the skin again, and drill holes for the spaces where the grommets would be attached.

They worked in small assembly-line groups, moving from one task to the next. We completed about a hundred linings a day (quite a few, when you consider it—close to a thousand of them a week), to the great satisfaction of the German inspectors.

THE CHIEF OFFICER CALLED ME in for a discussion about a month later. "Can you now organize the shipping of crates of these linings to Germany?"

I said, "Why not? I'm sure I can do it, once I get the proper dimensions."

A smile passed across his big, round face, lifting his heavy moustache and the massive eyebrows that hung like a precipice over his eyes. "Good! I was sure I could depend on you."

It was a gift from heaven. I began to show up in the crating area at about 5:00 a.m., at least an hour before anybody else got there, in order to create a clean workspace. That meant, to begin with, that I had to chase a horde of bigger and smaller rats out of the way. They were always there. I stamped my feet by way of notification, which acted like an alarm system for them—in a matter of seconds, they had all disappeared into the nooks and crannies of the building. Live and let live, I thought, as long as they didn't get in my way while I worked. And besides, they had their own important role to play in the Kurt Goldner war effort.

I always ordered lumber well in advance and had it ready to start the construction of the crates as soon as the workers appeared at 6:00 in the morning—we specialized in making two-by-four frames covered by wooden planks and, when everything else was done, we nailed on metal straps in both directions. The crates were about four feet by five, and about three and half feet high. We loaded them with great efficiency, each lining laid flat side by side with the others.

My rule about being on the job site an hour early had a second virtue, as I have just suggested, my contribution to the war: Once the crate was fully wrapped and I appeared alone in the early morning cold, I began to catch bunches of baby rats and slip them into the crates, between the folded materials. I was pretty confident those helmet linings would never arrive at their destination in usable condition.

AS FAR AS MY *LIFE* was concerned, the young crew I was hanging out with in my spare time had changed their hours to fit mine. We had a joyous time, actually. And I was for them a messenger of the future with the experiences of my past.

My parents wre managing wonderfully with the widow who owned the house we were living in. I was able to buy sufficient food with the money I earned, and I received a few bonuses as well from the Germans—who kept complimenting me on my success as a manager. The Jewish Society, comprised of indigent people of the village who were for some reason or other being allowed even in those later days of the war to function within the German system, was also very helpful to my parents with food and other necessities—blankets, socks, gloves, soles for shoes, and so on.

It's interesting that, when I was about thirteen and still living a normal life in Vienna, I had been sent to a dance school at which I had to wear a uniform, as did the girls. The boys' included white gloves. It was a rather military orchestration, but they were already teaching *avant garde* dances like the fox trot; naturally, the waltz was the jewel of the course, but after a half hour or so of that, the boys offered their arms to their partners, the girls threaded theirs through, and they had to promenade around the perimeter of the studio, which was not very far away from the riding academy for the Lippizaners. Years later, when I returned to Vienna in my fifties, the dance students were still wearing those gloves.

To bring these experiences to my young friends in Bacau—who, considering that times remained very hard, appear remarkably healthy and vibrant—was quite a revelation. There was conversation about politics and questions of how maybe to be able to plan a future in that still-desperate situation.

I was approached by a few somewhat more mature men who asked, in Yiddish, "Can we depend on you in the future, if we need you?"

They weren't like people trying to hurt me in some way; I couldn't mistrust them. "When the time comes," I said, "we'll see."

In relatively short order, I realized that they were part of the Russian underground. Two young guys approached me one night. "We need you to help us with something," one of them, a somewhat lower-class-looking fellow, not very well put together, his clothing and hair poorly cut, and not well shaven, said to me.

I said, "Sure. I'll be happy to. I can give you my time from Friday night to Sunday night—but I have to be sure to be back at my job on Monday morning. What do you need me for?"

His face, illuminated only on one side by the harsh bulb that was hanging from the ceiling, was grim. "We need somebody who looks and speaks German like a native. There's where you can be of great help to us. But we can't tell you exactly what will happen. There will be a program worked out."

I sighed, realizing where the talk was leading, said, "Okay," and shook hands with both of them.

THEY PICKED ME UP IN an old Chevrolet, and we drove about an hour and a half north.

Eventually, they pulled the car to the side of the road. A group of about eight men were standing there, milling around. They had an SS officer tied to a tree. When I came up, they ordered him to undress.

"I am a special part of my Führer's spirit!" he declared.

They seized the front of his tunic. "Take it off, damn you!"

I said to him in German, "Hear me out. There's

no point in trying to have a conversation with these people. If you don't do what they tell you, they'll shoot you—and if you have a family in Germany, *they'll* never know what happened to you. If you do what they say, I'll beg them to spare you. Do you hear me? You're an SS officer, and I'm a Jew who may be able to save your life. Don't forget that, ever!"

He blinked once and immediately undressed. They gave him some ragged clothing to wear instead.

The uniform fit me to a T. I said to them, "Make sure to keep my clothing in a package for me. I can't go back to Bacau as a *Schutzstaffel* officer."

"Yes, yes," said the leader of the group, a tough, bearded, unbelievably dirty man who looked for all the world as if he had lived in a cave for ten years. "Now, listen to me. You will bring us as your prisoners to the next German outpost. Your vehicle has broken down, and you need a translator for us who knows the special Russian dialect we speak, so you can extract information from us, since you believe we know something about Russian troop movements in a particular area. . . . Got it? . . . Okay, then. Let's try to get there by the earliest hour of the morning. The approach itself we will leave up to you to make convincing."

We let the officer go. I pointed the direction to go in, in order to save his life, and watched him disappear into the darkness. We had to walk quite a bit. They apparently knew the terrain that we had to traverse very well.

After resting crouched together for about an hour, the leader said, "Let's go. Pull out your revolver, and

My "war trophy"—the Iron Cross I removed from the German officer whose life I saved in Romania.

let's do it."

I marched them down the road to the outpost as a cold dawn was beginning to appear on the horizon.

Chapter 17

EIL *HITLER!*" I BARKED. WE had marched into a German military outpost—a big, boxlike building probably used to store ammunition. "Our vehicle broke down, and we need *Dolmetsch* to get necessary information from these people about troop movements."

"Whatever you want," said the young officer of some sort to whom I was speaking, with a totally washed-out personality. "We *have* no interpreters here, though. But I'm sure we have one at the next station."

I ordered my prisoners to sit against the wooden

walls as they had told me to do before we showed up there. We got a small bite of food to eat, cheese embedded in slices of bread.

As I was finishing a mouthful, I said to the young officer, "Please—time is of the essence in this matter. Can you arrange to prepare vehicles for us, and a driver to bring it back?"

IT TOOK ONLY A SHORT time before we got a transport vehicle just big enough to hold everybody. I ordered the men to climb into it, with appropriate shouts and hauteur. I briefly thanked the man in charge of the place, we saluted, and off we went. I was sitting next to the driver. I turned to the back, keeping a revolver visible on my lap.

A short time later, we heard a great explosion. The leader of the group whispered to me, "All right. It's time to take over."

I ordered the driver, virtually a teenager, slight of build and not yet developed or fully grown, to pull the truck off the road. He was completely confused by this, and even more so when he had pulled up the emergency brake and I ordered him to get out of his uniform. I said with a grim smile, "We'll give you some clothing, and then you take off and save your skin, you hear me?"

He repeated over and over, "I don't understand, I don't understand!"

"That will come later," I told him. "For now, just get out of here. Save your life. We're taking command of this vehicle."

The difference in appearance between my SS uniform and the raggedy prisoner's outfit we gave him completely confused the driver, but he did as I told him, obedient soldier that he was. My orders were not to be questioned, and I doubt he so much as suspected even by then that I was an imposter.

My companions were staring at me. "Let him go and save his life," I said flatly. They may not have liked it, but they did allow him to leave, and he went stumbling down the road in a half-stupor.

We all breathed a sigh of relief. I got out of my uniform and said that I had to return to the town I had come from as expeditiously as possible. They nodded and climbed back into the truck. "We buried the bombs between the wooden boards back there at the outpost," their leader told me as I joined them and we started off in the early light.

A couple of hours went by before they dropped me off on the outskirts of Bacau. I was worried most about my involvement with them remaining unknown. I felt I could trust them to say nothing (if I hadn't, I would never have embarked on the exercise), but one never knew. As the truck bumped and growled along those night roads in the darkness, the headlights throwing arcs of light through the emptiness all around us, I wondered, What if one of them gets captured and tortured? This is something I had to do—but what will happen then? . . .

They had, in any case, with my help, thus acquired in one night two military uniforms and a regulation German army vehicle, everything they needed for God only knew what.

I marched into town as quickly as I could and finally reached familiar terrain. It was pretty late in the morning by then—a Sunday. Some of the young people I knew started to ask where I had been. I avoided any response.

THE NEXT MORNING, I RETURNED to my helmet-lining department. I found it better not to discuss anything with anybody, certainly not what had happened over the weekend, or anything about my collaboration with baby rats in shipping crates—though anyone in my position would have reached the same conclusion, I am sure. The crates were sealed again, and a German military truck picked them up and drove away with them. I thought with grim pleasure for a moment of what some outpost in Russia would discover when they opened those crates, but then I forgot about it. There was work to be done.

The German officers said there were plans afoot to move the factories further south, since the Russian armies were approaching. This never happened, though. It took only a couple of weeks to discover that the helmet linings had been totally destroyed by hungry rats. The commandant was dismayed. I suggested that, probably, *metal* containers would offer greater protection, but the approval for that had to come from people higher up in the chain of command.

Once it became clear that the front was indeed collapsing back on Bacau, moreover, a great commotion went up among the occupying forces. The German troop levels certainly seemed to start shrinking after that.

ALL OF A SUDDEN ONE fine morning in the summer of
1944, they disappeared altogether—and the rumbling
noise of Russian troop carriers and great numbers of
marching solders came up the road and swarmed
over the terrain.

We had, my parents and I, improbably survived.

Plans for the future, I realized with a shock as I
watched the troop carriers roll past in the bright,
crisp fall light, needed to be formulated.

It was all part of the *motion* for me, of the problem of how to get from here to there. I felt some relief, of course—we had been running from the
Germans, I making myself useful as I could, indeed
living among them, for an awfully long time. But the
confusion that followed was enormous. My situation
had ceased to be lethal in the sense that some lunatic
in the SS could no longer shoot me down like a stray
dog. But nothing had otherwise become any more
certain. The factories, and every other enterprise in
town, were being taken over by the Russians.

In the encounters that followed, we heard constant
orders demanding, "*Davai chasei!*" which means, "Give
me your watch!" There were quite a few incidents of
rape of local women—very disappointing to the Jewish

people living there who looked on the Russians as liberators. Communication was very difficult too, even though locals knew Rutanian, a *patois* of Russian and Romanian.

I had a tough time as well creating a reliable pattern of life for myself and my parents. It was another kind of military occupation, and in some ways *worse* than it had been with the Wehrmacht—with them, I had achieved a certain accommodation. The Russians, who had taken over every facility to achieve a commanding position, offered me no opportunity to establish a similar arrangement.

Then, one day, I met a Russian officer—a man with a young face and very worried eyes, in the olive-green uniform with red trim of the regular army, whose entire expression was that of a very important person (though he may not have been) and who had a friendly manner, and we finally realized we could communicate in Yiddish.

He somehow discovered a few of the photographs that showed me restoring works of art, and he insisted that Russia would have great need of people like me to come and salvage the destruction that the Germans had caused. "It would be good for you, and it would be a blessing for my people," he added.

"I understand," I told him. "Truly, I do, and I would have no hesitation to join you and your people. But the most important thing I have to do now is to save my parents and try to help them survive. Do you see that?"

He nodded gravely. We were by then, my mother and I, already trying to find a way to communicate with Bucharest, a calm, occupied city at that time, the capital of the country.

Chapter 18

⌒☙⌒

I T TOOK A PRETTY LONG while to do so, but we got to Bucharest in the end. I had to arrange transportation—vehicles of various kinds and trains. It was no problem, though, once you knew how. The issue was somewhat complicated by the question of money. But help came from all sides: payments made for this or that by people who were trying to help us, individual Jews who had somehow, against all odds, managed to hold onto their money all through the German occupation.

Anyhow, the trip to Bucharest took a few days. We arrived in the spring of 1945. My parents were physically in pretty good shape then—a lot of time had elapsed since we dined on raw potato skins; more importantly, the notion of actually going to see their daughter again in America, distant as that prospect may then have been, lifted their spirits. My mother was sixty then, my father sixty-three.

I rented a room for us, with permission to use the kitchen facilities, in the center of town. Because I was able to speak some Romanian, I could also manage the day-to-day mechanics of living.

I met a female sculptor through mutual acquaintances who was related to one of the upper-crust inhabitants of Bacau and who had settled in the capital and had a small studio for her work. She was a beautiful young woman—dark haired and tall, with a beautiful figure she made efforts to play down in the way she dressed. She was Jewish too, highly educated, and pursuing a pretty successful career in clay that was eventually cast in bronze or aluminum. Her husband traveled a great deal, though I never knew for what purpose. I offered to pose as a model for her. She was very pleased, and we grew close. She seemed to be able to speak my language—the language, that is to say, of an artist, a dialect I had not spoken for all practical purposes since my time in the Academie.

She gave some thought to my rather precarious situation and soon introduced me to one of the important people in the Bucharest Museum, a man who had assembled a substantial collection for the king. He was a youngish fellow who resembled so many employed by large organizations—well dressed, well mannered, and remarkably unenthusiastic about the future so unclear as yet while the government went through a series of upheavals, forming and reforming.

We met in his office in the museum, a very bare, large space with good lighting. "It's a tough situation, you see," he complained. "There are no experienced people around in the field of restoration. I'd be thrilled to have you work for me."

". . .Well, yes," I said, "I'd be happy to. But my main purpose is to get out of the country and aim for the future that I and my parents have been deprived of for, well, you know, a pretty long time. . .everything depends on bribes, everything, the solution to every problem."

"I can understand that," he said, "and I haven't even figured out the answers to how to solve those issues in my *own* life. . . . Anyhow, we understand each other, then. But let me give you some work in the meantime."

I did do some work for him, but everything accumulated, all kinds of pressures. I was totally involved in one love affair after another with women. There was a famous pianist among them; there were Romanians and internationals, Christians and Jews (neither they nor I had any religious limitations). This occupied a lot of my time, though I can't claim to have complained about it at the time.

THROUGH THE SCULPTRESS, I MET a person who was destined to change my life. Her name was Sofia Abramovici (she had adopted another last name, Bramura, of course, as I had and so many others, to avoid being easily identifiable as Jewish). Small and very good-looking, she was in her mid-twenties, the youngest of three sisters. She had widely spaced, dark eyes in a perfectly oval face, and a straight nose above a full, wide mouth, framed by very dark hair. The eyes were expressive, alive, full of intensity. She was constantly busy producing high-quality custom lampshades with her two sisters. The sisters were still living with her parents and had a workshop there. Sofia herself had just acquired a miniature duplex penthouse apartment in the center of Bucharest. I made an appointment to meet her there. I had come to discuss what might be possible for me to do in a constructive way to make some money.

It was during the afternoon, the weather sunny, white clouds scudding across a powder-blue sky.

She was very businesslike. "I understand you're looking for work. The question is, How can I integrate you into the work we do? Maybe you can. . . would you be interested in doing some murals in houses I work in? I have one right now, for example. They want an interpretation of Breugel's *Wedding Feast*, a wall in a dining area. Could you do that?"

"Yes, certainly. I've done murals before."

In most cases, as I have mentioned, women had been approaching me since I arrived in Bucharest; they were all in the arts in one way or another, liberated, as was the country—as was of course the world. I was basically a shy fellow who had never learned to make the first move.

Sofia was not like that. She was herself reserved, even aloof, and hardly took the initiative or even signaled—as some women do instead—an interest.

She had studied the arts in Paris and acquired a considerable knowledge of fashion design. Her hard accent had somehow slowed down her relations in Paris, but she still had contact with some people in the French Embassy in Bucharest, which would be very helpful later on when we arrived in Paris together.

Eventually, I overcame my reticence with Sofia and made the first move. We became lovers. It didn't take long for us to get much more deeply involved than that.

ONE DAY, I FELT I needed to talk to her about my plans for the future. She had not as yet met my parents, though she knew I was living with them; I had met her sisters, who resented my appearance in the family *milieu*, as it were.

I cleared my throat and said, "Sofia, we have to talk. Things are getting serious between us, but I must find a way to move to America. That's the future for me and my mother and father."

Without much hesitation, in her typical way, she smiled and said, "Well, then, I'll go with you. It will mean leaving my parents and sisters, but you are *my* future. Agreed?"

I was dumbfounded by the simplicity of this response. She was a woman of enormous clarity, enormous character. "First," she said, "we must make plans to go to Paris."

The U.S. Embassy had just opened an office in Bucharest. The war was over in that late summer of 1945, but, again, nothing was clear; paths of movement were still murky for all of us refugees from the years before it had started.

I put on my suit, well brushed, and a clean shirt and tie, and went to the U.S. Embassy, a small office set up in a commercial building. A young man spoke to me—an extraordinarily handsome one who looked like a movie star in a well-cut suit, a conservative tie, and a cigarette. "Sorry for the appearance of the place," he began, brushing back a lock of straight blond hair from his forehead, after shaking my hand. "This is all temporary. . . . What can I do for you?"

"I want to arrange for a visa to the United States for my parents."

He asked me some questions about our situation

and then leaned back in his chair and said, "Well, with their son-in-law, your sister's husband, serving in the armed forces, this will be a fairly easy thing to arrange. You have to make your way to Paris, where you'll find the necessary papers in our embassy there, and they can leave after that."

Chapter 19

SOFIA AND I ACCORDINGLY PUT my parents on a train to Paris. They were dressed in carefully preserved clothing from the past, he in a suit and tie, she in a dark ladies' suit.

They had had to acquire an exit visa from the Romanian authorities, which involved a payoff in cash to the right official. Sofia's friend, a lawyer, had explained to us, "I'll arrange it for you. Here's the way it will work. You go next Monday to the Ministry of the Interior, third floor, and see a Mr. Mihalescu. He will have a chair next to his desk. You sit down on that chair. He'll open a drawer. You drop in an envelope that contains an amount I will tell you to put in it, and he'll turn over the visas for your parents and for you and Sofia."

But since we were already busy with doing interior design work and making various arrangements to leave, I had sent my father instead. He'd followed my instructions to the letter—but, being the uncompromisingly honest man that he was, after he slipped the envelope full of Romanian currency into Mihalescu's open drawer and accepted the four exit visas in exchange, he had proceeded, in all innocence, to ask for a written receipt.

The official had almost fainted upon hearing this. "What do you mean?" he'd asked.

"Well, I want to make sure that my son has transferred the proper amount to the proper people."

Mihalescu had shouted, "Get out of here as fast as you can!"

Mother and Father were almost in a trance by then, having survived seven years of constant tension and uncertainty. They were older, of course, and thinner, though, according to my calculations, my mother was only about sixty—a very young person still in today's terms, though sixty seemed old to me then.

I had been managing their lives since the moment I had reunited with them in 1941. All I'd cared about was that they should survive the war, though I had no even moderately safe plan for achieving that goal and had taken whatever chances I had to as we moved along, hoping eternally for the best. I did not yet feel I had succeeded at this, despite the end of the war—I wanted to see them out of Europe and the still-considerable uncertainties that we were facing. My mother mumbled constantly, "I want to see my daughter again!" Coca and her husband had by then been living in New York for five years.

As I watched the train pull out of the Bucharest station with a great hiss of steam that rolled down the platform and a high-pitched whine of a whistle, I could only think, *Another miracle!* I wished I knew how to say a prayer of thanks to have thus witnessed the impossible become reality, but I had never learned any prayers, had no knowledge of my Jewish traditions whatsoever, and had not yet found a plausible solution to the great puzzle of how a God could exist who would permit such things as I had lived through to happen. . .and I had lived through far, far less than millions of others.

SOFIA AND I PREPARED TO cross the border from Romania into Hungary—it was the closest one and the nearest way of getting transportation to the West. We were aiming to meet my parents in Paris. As I have said, we had the necessary exit visas but no papers. We were what was called "stateless." So we crossed illegally, finding a little town named Battovia, which was inhabited by Germans who had settled there some time before and which straddled the border— half Romanian, that is, and half Hungarian, so that all we had to do was stroll from one end of town to the other in order to achieve our purpose.

Very close beyond there, we reached another little town where we were able to buy tickets to Vienna with some German currency we had. That took about a day. We wandered through the town, considering the old-fashioned (perhaps primitive) houses that seemed to have escaped all contact with modernity and to be languishing still in some early-nineteenth-century fog, though a war had just come and gone. . . .

There was, at least, plenty of food everywhere in Hungary. We ate their salami and bread, drank some local white wine, light and satisfying, and boarded the train with a growing sense of optimism.

When we reached Vienna, I again tracked down the businessman father of my former schoolmate, the one who had introduced me to the Kunsthistorisches Museum it seemed an eternity before, to see if he could suggest how to get further west. I showed up at his apartment on the corner of Josefstädterstrasse.

The apartment hadn't changed much. He, however, seemed to have aged considerably in the intervening years, and appeared much frailer than I remembered.

My problem was that, since the Russians had occupied the eastern regions of Austria, crossing the border to the western part—which was occupied by the Americans and from which I could travel to Paris or any other destination—required a valid reason to do so. I asked him what I should do. He nodded thoughtfully, went to his desk, and composed a few letters. "This will help, just in case," he said, handing them to me. "With your accent, though, there will be no question of residency, so I'm sure they'll let you through. What excuse are you going to give them?"

"That I have to be in Salzburg on family business," I replied.

"Good. That will work fine. And then we can get Sofia to you somehow."

She could not come with me because her *r-r-r* accent was too strong, and every foreign language became a caricature for her.

As it turned out, nobody even asked me what my plans were in crossing into the western half of the country—I boarded the train, and that was that.

We had learned that a known displaced persons camp existed in Salzburg that I had no intention of entering. Instead, I rented a small room in the vicinity of the camp, visited it, and made many acquaintances with the people there, driven by a powerful urge to acquaint myself with survivors, with as many people as I could find who had in some way or other shared the life I had been leading since that bomb destroyed my paintings in Antwerp. In an unavoidable fashion, I was no longer entirely at ease in the presence of people who had not been driven, like me, to endure, to overcome absurdly unlikely odds.

The neighborhood of the camp, on the periphery of the city, was more rural than urban, composed of nondescript white houses surrounded by kitchen gardens.

I sent then for Sofia; the Viennese businessman acquired some authentic peasant garb for her and was planning to drive her to Salzburg as soon as was practicable, presenting her as a country relative.

There were many children there who had survived the war in monasteries and convents. They were brought to the camp completely unaware of the war's end. Some of them were still screaming, "My name is Christian! Schmidt! And I am Catholic!"

And there were psychiatrists there who told them that, no, they were Jewish, that their parents had placed them in those Christian religious establishments to save them, that now they could reconnect with their Jewish heritage and take up where their lives had been shattered. That sort of thing happened over and over.

I MET ONE YOUNG MAN in the camp who was leading a division of the Irgun in Austria. He looked like a teenager but was probably in his late twenties then, sophisticated as a college student, dark haired, dark eyed, and cleanly shaven. At that moment, the Irgun was planning reprisals against the British, in Europe as well as in Palestine. Jews were trying to immigrate to Palestine in small ships. The English were intercepting these vessels whenever they could and shipping the refugees to Cyprus, where they had established detention camps for them, cooperating with the Arabs in general to keep the Jews out under an agreement with the Arab League—as if the Balfour Declaration, recognizing the right of the Jews to a state of their own, had not been issued in 1926.

The young man asked me one day to carry some packages up into the mountains for him. There was an abandoned shack up there where a connection had been established with the Irgun. It was amazing, I thought. Nothing was impossible for these Jews.

I told him I would do it.

Chapter 20

I WAS PRETTY SURE THAT the package contained explosives. The materials had been shoved into a pack large enough to cover my entire back. It was heavy, but I traveled by local bus to a station in the foothills, from which I started to march up into the mountains. It was the fall of '45, sunny and not cold but windy, though I was oblivious to all that. I was all alone in a long-sleeved shirt, pants, and a scarf around my neck. I had no boots, just the one pair of shoes I owned.

I passed many local people on my way who waved to me again and again, assuming that I was one of their soldiers, and asked, "When did you get back from Russia?"

"Just a few days ago," I invariably replied.

"Thank god you're here."

I started yodeling to fit in with the environment. If I had been wearing *lederhosen*, it would have been perfect.

It was a very steep march up those alpine stretches. I had a bottle of water with me and a few slices of bread to keep me going. It took me a whole day to reach the meeting place, a broken-down shack that looked almost as if it was drowning in the landscape.

I opened the creaking, ramshackle door. Everything inside was broken down. It was a complete ruin—the walls fractured, beams of the ceiling collapsed, rubble everywhere. There were no windows.

A young man somewhat older than I, in worn clothing, a jacket and heavy pants that didn't match, was waiting in the shadowy gloom. He was unshaven. I didn't quite comprehend what he was saying, but he must have been informed that I was coming, because he seemed to have expected me. He came toward me and embraced me. I said, "In case you have some control over it, for my own peace of mind—my thoughts have tormented me all the way walking up here—I want to ask you to mount the explosives on the abyss side of the track, so the train will be thrown against the mountain instead of falling over the edge. That ought to be enough, in any case, to achieve your purpose. The message will be the same."

"What you're asking," he said after a long moment, "is totally against our policy in these matters . . .but they'll take it into consideration."

I asked how they communicated among themselves, but he said, "That is of no consequence, and anyhow, you don't need to know. Don't worry about it. We have our ways."

WITHOUT THE WEIGHT ON MY back and going downhill, I felt relieved by the request I had made, but I wasn't sure if what I had asked for was constructive to the drive and spirit of that fighting organization. The moonlight aided my descent, since by then the sun had set and it was growing colder. I marched until midnight before I reached a little village; the whole place seemed asleep; I tucked myself into a depression in the landscape and slept until I heard the first noises of activity waken me, and I asked for information on how to return to Salzburg from some elderly men who had begun to appear on the street.

What they told me sounded very simple, but they made it clear to me that it was quite a distance to walk. I hardly cared about that.

On and off, a vehicle would pass me on the road and, when I waved it down, give me a lift convenient to the driver's destination. In this fashion, I returned to the Salzburg DP camp in the late afternoon. I found the clean-shaven youngster who had sent me off on my journey and told him I had done what he asked. He held my right hand in both of his until we parted company.

A day later, I had a complicated conversation in English with an American officer in a special location outside the camp, on the outskirts of Salzburg, perhaps a former military compound. The U.S. military was handling the whole maintenance of the DP camp.

He was very handsome in his crisp uniform, and he chose very short words to make me understand him. Something fishy was going on with food deliveries, and it disturbed me, though it meant little to everybody else in the camp because there was no starvation. I asked him, "How does it happen that the food deliveries to the DP camp come somewhat later than they appear on the black market?"

He gave me a withering look. "The percentage," he said, "is more than adequate for the inhabitants of your camp."

That ended the conversation.

A FEW DAYS WENT BY before Sophie arrived as my friend in Vienna had promised, dressed in her local-looking peasant garb. We settled for a few days in my rented room, so we could explain what had happened to each other, and we planned our departure for Paris.

I have said that I felt a real need to meet as many survivors of the war as I could, that I felt a deep affinity with what they had been through, but there was more to this feeling. It was of course true that "others" had not shared our terrors, our griefs and small triumphs; it was also true, however, that I was always troubled by what these others had in fact done in the war, how they had comported themselves. Had they been part of the vicious enemy whose grasp I and my parents, and tens of thousands of others, had been so driven to escape, those who had killed so many of my fellow Jews out of hatred or greed or sheer stupidity; or had they been among those (fewer in number, to be sure, but enough to save very, very many) who had looked the other way at a crucial moment in some poor refugee's life?

As long as they said nothing, I concluded, I would not ask.

I was also confused by the relationship some of the American soldiers had with the locals—the fraternization that half a pack of cigarettes could buy a man. They seemed, in their own way, to be preying on helpless humanity in a manner not unlike that of the Germans, the Austrians, the Poles. . .but people were not dying, I reminded myself. This was better.

There was train service from Salzburg to Paris. No papers were required, only the money to pay for the tickets. I still had some left from Romania, and Sophie still had all of hers as well that she had exchanged into francs and marks. She of course knew my parents by then. It was just a matter of getting packed and ready to leave.

This we did in short order.

Part Three

A KIND OF FREEDOM

Chapter 21

SOPHIE AND I REACHED Paris by train in the spring of 1946. The city was a glorious example of a busy, self-important hive of activity—like a female movie star who is entirely conscious of her beauty, inner light, and ability to move others to adoration. The entrances to every building expressed its importance in beauty of line and richness of structure. We were both mesmerized by this, and by the fact that the French appeared not to pay much attention to this grandeur—they took it, they took *everything*, for granted: Theirs was the artistic and culinary center of the known universe, the pinnacle of civilized life, and they wore this knowledge with what they, I imagine, thought of as negligent grace, *noblesse oblige* in an egalitarian age.

We were plunged almost immediately into being busy and in demand, a heartbeat that seemed to last for many, many years to come.

We somehow discovered *our* importance for the first time through Sophie's very substantial business awareness. She knew how to pry money loose from the world around her and flourish.

I was soon preoccupied with overcoming the details of our involvement, even to the point of refreshing the palace of Baron de Hogue, who, ten years later, came to New York, when we were living there, with several antique objects that might, he thought, be transformed into lamp bases.

In his opinion, America was already highly advanced, and he thought it would be a fine idea to create very complicated lampshades for each of the bases.

The palace I am speaking of was located in one of the great *arrondissements* in the near vicinity of the Arc de Triomphe. We met him through a gentleman named Roger, who was the editor-in- chief of

Hachette, a rather grand and very well-established publishing house. Sophie knew him from the time when he represented the firm in Bucharest. He was a tall, elegant fellow, very French, his hair beautifully combed, his haberdashery in the finest repair. His French was impeccable, and she had catered to his needs in Romania—translating for him, making it possible for him to function. He was returning the favor to her and me.

Interestingly enough, I had a few tubes of oil paint left from Bucharest, and, having found a small piece of wood from the back of an armoire in the lodging we had found when we first arrived, I painted a somber landscape of about two feet by one and a half that had a post-Impressionist feel to it, and that resulted in an encounter with a man who said he could absolutely use it and wanted a dozen more with different trees in various locations that he could promote throughout France and order more as they sold.

I never got his name because, at that point, I told him, "Sorry—I'm not a machine," which was the wrong response. He dropped the subject instantly, and Sophie took my response as important; it would have been a very beneficial kind of enterprise, but the variety of other possible occupations for me was so enormous and so incredible, even to my mind, that I felt I didn't have to trap myself in that way, and neither did she. I could hardly have expected to respond to every project that came my way. I had gone from being a useless drag on the world to pretty much the very opposite. In addition, being Jewish was totally irrelevant as a barrier to work, as was being a refugee.

De Hogue's limestone home—an *hôtel particulier* that was perhaps two hundred years old at the time and had an inner courtyard with beautiful gardens, tall windows, and a marble figure emerging from the grassy surround in the middle of it—needed some restoration of the physical spaces. Roger arranged a meeting with the baron; we went there together, Sophie and I.

De Hogue was a true gentleman—slim, tallish, with a rather distant manner, very well dressed and with impeccable manners. He met us himself at the front door and led us around the house, pointing out what he thought needed to be done, and surprised when I suggested how I would handle the work and supervise it—which was an even greater surprise to me, since I had never done such a thing before and had no notion of how I would.

He was silent at that meeting regarding the question of how much this restoration work would cost or how long it would take, leaving to us the issue of working out such details.

Naturally, I had for the first time in my professional life to engage artisans who would execute my ideas. The first was a general contractor I found when someone gave me his address and I looked him up. He was a Frenchman with whom I got along very well and who knew everybody else in the trade, and through him I gradually found workmen of all kinds. His name was Philippe, and he looked like a contractor—slightly worn clothing, poor teeth, very big hands, and a mustache surrounded by a generally unshaven face. He allowed me to guide him with my requirements and sketches; his response was invariably informative, and he taught me a great deal.

And his physical appearance, like that of so many of his fellow craftsmen, had nothing remotely to do with the achievements they could attain with their labor, or the stream of advice that issued from their mouths and that was enormously helpful to me. I had, you understand, what you might perhaps call a good eye for the work, imagination, a sense of the creative that is indispensable for anyone who wants to build a home for others to live in, but none of the mechanical skills to render those strengths in wood and stone and fabric. Without those slightly disheveled, patient, and hard-working men, I could never have gotten my fledgling efforts off the ground.

A small incident illustrates this. A young couple came to me with a request for a shelf for their telephone. I came to their *garçonnière*—their efficiency apartment—to see what they were talking about. I was somehow overwhelmed by the emptiness of the place, but I picked a spot on the wall and said, "A shelf is really not sufficient for me to get involved, but when you talk on the telephone, it would be a good idea to have a mirror on the wall above it, so you can look at yourself while you're talking. Do you have a table?"

"No," said the very young woman, barely out of her teens. "Not yet."

"Well," I told her, "if we place that mirror on a wooden panel and hinge it well so that it can come down, and hinge two legs to what will then become the underside and can come out and snap into place, you can have a table any time you need one."

Discussing this idea with Phillipe, I came up with an interesting item, finished all around, that I have repeated countless times since, with the same telephone shelf under it in symbolic memory—rather stylish, it has traveled through Empire, Chinese, modern, and various other incarnations.

My inventiveness, as it were, had such great success, surprising both my clients as well as myself, that it encouraged me to suggest many other things to embellish and bring practical use to the lives of my clients. I have been doing such things ever since—including credenzas twelve inches deep that opened up into a single bed, behind which was tucked a hinged night stand and a reading lamp; screens that carried all kinds of decorations that would fit a finished wall and that opened up to reveal little efficiency kitchens (many years later, doing a house for one of my clients, an Orthodox Jewish rabbi, I refused to construct a Passover kitchen, as was common, in the basement. I replaced it with a big mirrored table, with extensions, and squeezed a tiny kitchen into a recess in the breakfast nook); on the outside of these screens I often placed engravings that made the screen look like a finished wall.

Phillipe's enthusiastic response to all of my ideas involved detail and finish work, at which he was very good. It became a ping-pong game between us that I have often happily repeated with other contractors, and in other fields. Many years later, I found a cabinet maker in New York, a very short man, maybe the shortest I have ever met, who was always bundled up and had the memory of a moustache and a beard about him, named Père Villard. He was disregarded and merely given small repair jobs by the public, largely because he couldn't understand English and very few of his potential clientele spoke French. I realized that he was yet another enthusiastic craftsman, and we shared a lot of joy and life for years.

My first clients recommended me to others, who recommended me to others still, and in this way, as I suppose is most always the case, the business grew.

Chapter 22

M Y FUNCTION IN THOSE DAYS was always defined by the obligations that were being thrown at me by each client, who by and large differed from all the others and presented unique challenges, especially at that moment in my career when I had so little experience in dealing with such clients.

One of my great resources was the antiques markets of Paris, the Marché aux Puces and the Marché Biron. They were located in a district of many blocks at the very end of the Metro, with some stalls in the open air, under makeshift covers, for those people who were transients, and indoor places for the more stable companies that had been there for a long time.

When you emerged from the subway station, you encountered various entrances to the different markets. Certain dealers were in one area, others in another. The streets were still in part cobblestoned, and the buildings were really wooden shacks with tin roofs. There was nothing *vieux Paris* about the place, though, nothing Eugene Atget would have been aroused by as a photographer. The proprietors, however, were all French. They had all managed to survive the war one way or another, and the Jews among them spoke no Yiddish and weren't like any Jews I had ever known.

The discovery in these markets of the precious remnants of prior centuries immediately influenced me to incorporate them into my design activities, as well as in their application to newly created pieces— a small, broken miniature chest, say, that soon became part of ten- or twelve-foot armoire. My goal was to make such marriages look as if they had been there together forever.

It was only later, when we were already living in America, that we came back to refresh our sources of inspiration in the same markets, though the people were always changing. We were often recognized in those later years, but we recognized very few of these entrepreneurs.

I would spend whole days wandering through those streets. I had no preexisting notion of what I "needed" for some clients or other; my goal was to be surprised by what I found. There was a variety of sources in the markets, businesses that specialized in certain items—small statuary, bronze applications, furniture fragments, artwork in an assortment of mediums, sources for lamps, chandeliers, and sconces, mostly gilt bronze. Other shops specialized in certain periods, including the 18th and 19th centuries.

My problem then was that I had neither the time nor the funds to store an inventory of items—anything I bought I had either to store with Phillipe or deliver to a client—but Paris is a city of small, tight habitations, and only a small percentage of the population consists of the very rich. I had therefore to be extremely selective in what I bought at the markets. For immediate use, I only chose pieces we could absolutely incorporate in our designs. I found, for example, wooden pieces to use in a newly designed chest or table, to give it the flavor of provenance, the look and feel, of a previous age.

My major warfare in furniture style came much later, in America, when I had to overcome all the British influences, mostly Regency, that were all the rage then in New York. My motto was always to create something unique, literally, that nobody else had yet, with the flavor and styling of French culture.

English furniture, to my eye, was always stiff and choking on its own stiffness. French pieces were, by contrast, more flowing and friendlier, and altogether created an ambience in which it was possible to live, to be, that is, *human* in. English pieces set out to impress; French, to engage.

I used to go to the markets whenever I had a free moment. We either stuck to one particular area or raced through from one end to the other every few days, and we witnessed all the latest developments.

There was a division between average antique pieces and new copies, and, on the other hand, the very, very expensive antique stores carrying totally restored and reupholstered pieces with real provenance, and looking for American buyers who would totally disregard the prices. My clients, by contrast, were French people who were tight with money, always looking for a good deal. I did the work itself and handled the buying too, for which I paid cash (there was no other way); Sophie took charge of the billing, so that I never quite knew how much she sold things for, or how she charged people for my services as a designer.

THE YEARS PASSED VERY QUICKLY, jumping from one project to the next. I continued to buy the bargains at the markets; to me, the discovery of quality was all that mattered. I wasn't interested in getting polished, completed objects. I looked for something at which my eye would tell me, *This has possibilities! I can do things with this.* (The first home that I made in America, for a woman named Margie, was given to us in a bare state, and, in the spirit of Paris, we used in every way an antique piece that was exciting: A vase could become an end table, Roman or Egyptian bits find their way into another table and then be covered with glass, or a piece of antique tapestry be embedded in a wall. (She told me, when she sold her home many years later and moved to Florida, how hungry the antiques dealers were for what she had to sell, and how much they had been willing to pay.)

I also preoccupied myself with some restoration, but only small pieces, because my living quarters were so cramped I didn't have the space to work on larger ones.

We remained in Paris until 1950. In those four years, I had had to overcome French chauvinism— they were always trying to diminish you, in much the same way as Americans called anyone who came here to the States (and still do, I think) "greenhorns." One French doctor asked me my approach to cleaning paintings. I said there was always an addition of alcohol in the process. "Alcohol is a daily liquid in my professional life," he said. "I don't need to be told anything about it." He said nothing further on the matter until we got a panicked message from him: *Come immediately. It's very important*, and, when I reached his apartment, I saw a beautiful 17th-century Dutch painting on the table, surrounded by bottles of alcohol, and I threw myself immediately onto the painting with my sleeve and handkerchief, and any other material I could lay my hands on, to remove the alcohol, which had already stripped away great portions of the it.

"I *told* you," I said in some irritation, "alcohol

was only a *component* of this process, and that it var-
ied from piece to piece. Your use of it here was so
dominating, and your disregard of any other compo-
nents so complete, because you thought you knew all
about the stuff, that, when you applied it here, it took
over!"

"Your sense of what's important is different from
mine," he said in a distinctly cool tone of voice. "I
have to rethink our relationship."

Aside from that, those four years were like being
in a hectic period of study. By approaching everything as something new that I had to learn, and instantly traveling from one domain into the next,
giving little time to contemplation of my own life—
by going from mere day-to-day survival, in short, to
having a business, a wife, an ongoing need to do business and exercise my skills as an artist—I grew up
quickly.

Chapter 23

N 1950, MY MOTHER WROTE me a letter from New York in which she said, *The years are passing so fast, I want to make sure that I will see you again before I leave. Will you come to me?*

When I saw those words, I told Sofia, "The call from Momma has reached us. Let's finish all our obligations here, and let's go to America."

"I don't speak a word of English," she told me after our eyes met and a moment's thought. "The atmosphere might be very strange to me. . .but wherever you go, I go."

Then came the phase of saying goodbye to the

people in Paris who had been so supportive of all our efforts against the spirit of chauvinism in that luminous city. Sophie went from one to the next to offer our thanks and found people astonished by the news that we were leaving; but Roger said, "I want to talk to him."

I went to his office in early February, on a chilly pre-spring morning. "I thought you were doing so well here," he said. "Perhaps I should have recommended more clients to you—but, in the meantime, I want you to take several thousand francs to ease the financial pressure on you—and no interest and no time limit when you can repay me."

The very notion that a Frenchman would part with money, unless you cut off his fingers, immediately arose in my mind. I was almost shocked by the offer.

"It isn't the money," I explained. "It's the call of the family."

"...Where are you planning to go, then? Brazil? Mexico? Canada? Or *Etats Unis*?"

"Yes, the last. I'm going to America."

He looked at me with sorrow in his eyes. "It is a country with no civilization or culture," he whispered. "You will not be happy there."

But, *fait accompli,* he accepted my decision.

A few months followed, during which we completed our projects and packed our belongings. We were very well situated by then financially.

One day in late summer, we took a train to Le Havre and a ferry across the Channel to Southampton, where we met the *Queen Mary.* The weather was sunny and warm, and promising. We found our cabin and remained isolated, except for meals, for the next week.

When we reached the harbor of New York and beheld Manhattan, I was enormously eager to acquaint myself with the Statue of Liberty. We passed right by it to get to Ellis Island, where, after we disembarked, we were separated, which I greatly resented; a customs officer wanted to know why I had brought a very large bottle of Chanel #5 for my brother-in-law. Later, when required to give information about myself, I asked for a translator, someone in French or Yiddish. They wanted to know where we were coming from, what our purpose was in coming to America, and how we expected to make a living here. I knew some English, of course, but I stuck to the Yiddish I had learned in the Ukraine.

We had a presentation in front of a judicial official the following morning. When he had gone through his bureaucratic routine, he said, "Now you may look at the Statue of Liberty."

"I won't do that," I said to him, "through a prison window."

I don't know how much of this the translator actually conveyed.

Call it luck, call it Kismet—we entered the melting pot of New York in the U.S.A., among the few who were able to return to life.

PHOTO GALLERY

I'm the goalie of this soccer team in June 1936, Vienna

Riding a horse in the summer of 1936 in Bucovina

On an excursion in the Alps, summer 1936

With classmates in July 1936. The fellow second from the left, Bill Hargitay, later became the father of TV star Marissa Hargitay.

With a relative on a street in Bucovina, August 1937

Brussels, September 1939

In a field, Summer 1939

Brussels, September 1939

Identity card photograph, 1939

*With a friend at the beach during my tenure
at the Academie des Beaux Arts, 1939*

With friends from the Academie, 1939

Biking on the outskirts of Antwerp, 1939

A tranquil moment at the Academie des Beaux Arts.
I am fifth from the left.

Summer 1939

With friends from the Academie, Fall 1939

On the outskirts of Antwerp, 1939

With friends from the Academie, 1939

With two young friends, Brussels, Setember 1940

On the roof of our apartment building, Vienna, 1941

Embracing my mother, Vienna 1941

Listening to the radio with my parents, June 1941

With my uncle, Kommercialrat Berthold Storfer, 1941

The young crowd in Bacau, 1944. I am third from the left.

With friends in from of a stage set I had created, 1944.
I am second from the left.

Sofia, Paris, 1946

A NOTE ON THE FONT

This book has been set in Sabon, an old-style serif typeface with a very French feeling designed by the German-born typographer and designer Jan Tschichold (1902–1974) in the period 1964–1967. Design of the roman is based on types by Claude Garamond (c.1480–1561), particularly a specimen printed by the Frankfurt printer Konrad Berner. The italics are based on types designed by a contemporary of Garamond's, Robert Grandjon. Sabon is frequently described as a Garamond revival. The display face is Neutraburg, which echoes in its elegant sans-serif lines the design feeling of Bauhaus Europe.